The Psychology of Chess

DEDICATED TO
THE MEMORY OF
C.H.O'D.ALEXANDER

The Psychology of Chess

W.R. HARTSTON and P.C. WASON

Facts On File Publications
New York, New York ● Bicester, England

THE PSYCHOLOGY OF CHESS

© W. R. Hartson, P. C. Wason 1983, 1984
First published in the United States of America by
Facts on File, Inc., 460 Park Avenue South,
New York, NY 10016

First published in Great Britain by B. T. Batsford Limited

Library of Congress Cataloging in Publication Data

Hartston, William Roland, 1947-
  The psychology of chess.

  Bibliography: p.
  Includes index.
  1. Chess—Psychological aspects. I. Wason, P. C.
(Peter Cathcart) 11. Title.
GV1448. H37   1984   794.1′01′9   84-4113
ISBN 0-87196-226-8

Printed and bound in Great Britain

Contents

1 Introduction

This is a book about all you have ever wanted to know about chess players and never been afraid to ask. The answers certainly do not fall into a neat package, but we shall try to impose a little order on them even if we do not de-mystify too much.

The book should interest three classes of individuals. First, there are those people, who may be casual players, and who are fascinated both by the higher reaches of chess and by the thought processes which occur during play. If they play chess at all they do so as a relaxation. We make no apologies to them because most of what we have to say will probably be new. Second, there are those ardent players who participate in tournaments, or matches, or play serious correspondence chess. We crave their indulgence for repeating facts about chess and its exponents with which they may be all too familiar, but hope even here that they will come across some new things which will interest them. They are probably unlikely to know much about the psychological research which has been done. Third, there are the professional psychologists and their students, who know about the higher mental processes (thinking, remembering and perceiving), but who may not know much about chess. Their bonus will be knowledge about playing chess at the expense of the repetition of familiar problems.

We might ask at this point what the player, unversed in psychology, is likely to expect from this book. When we have mentioned this project both of us have encountered remarks like: "Oh, I'll show you a very interesting psychological incident which happened in my game'. We suspect that the connotations of the word 'psychology' are quite firmly fixed in the minds of the layman, and that they are radically deviant from those of the academic psychologist. For example, a player will tell us that he is likely to lose to x, who is objectively weaker than him, or to beat y, who is objectively stronger. Correspondence players (and not only correspondence players) have been known to fear players from a particular country even if they have no such anxieties about players from a country generally recognized as objectively stronger. Someone will point out that a particular move was intended to have a psychological effect. Another will be furious when an opponent adopts the Petroff Defence to his 1 e4, thus evading the more frequent Ruy Lopez, and seeming to have a drawish intent. All this would be psychology to the layman.

What characterizes each of these examples is that the behaviour in question deviates in some way from an expectation. One would not expect to lose to x or to beat y - it goes against an objective assessment of skill. One would not expect a player to be in awe of (say) Austrians, and to play without such inhibition against (say) Yugoslavs. One would not expect a weaker move to be played knowingly. Psychological? Perhaps. But in fact the main subject matter of the discipline of psychology is normal behaviour - how we learn to perceive the environment, or make simple movements, or draw inferences from given premises. How such behaviour is conceived, or rather how we develop theories about it, is at the moment extremely complex. And it is all the more so when it is remembered that psychology may be seen as struggling for identification between the sister sciences of linguistics, physiology and sociology. But whatever we say about this, the layman is likely to remain convinced that psychology is primarily concerned with exceptions to a norm, or with distortions of thought induced by some underlying cause. Conversely, of course, the psychologist, trapped in a social gathering, tends to dismiss the eager questions of the layman, perhaps in order to keep the questioner at a distance. A more balanced view, which naturally we hold, is that the kind of questions which obsess the layman should be tackled, if at all possible, by a systematic enquiry of an empirical kind.

Within the sphere of chess it is no accident that the most distinguished research has been conducted inside the laboratory, and has been concerned with the explanation of the way in which a master sees a chess position in a different way from an expert. These studies constitute a dominating influence in research on chess thinking. We consider them in Chapter 5, 'The Essential Patterns'.

The reason that such studies have been so prolific is because psychologists have conceptualized chess as the ideal intellectual task with which to investigate the way in which information is perceived, transformed and retained in relation to a dominating plan or goal. The results in some respects can be extrapolated to domains other than chess.

On the other hand, research on why people play chess, and what keeps them at it, is more speculative and lacking in cohesion. Here we turn to a different tradition within psychology – a tradition which the layman usually equates with 'psychology'. This is the field of dynamic psychology (or 'depth psychology') associated with the names of Freud and his followers. Analysts talk a totally different language from experimental psychologists and cognitive scientists, and the scientific status of their theories is highly controversial. Such theories have exerted a profound effect upon the humanities (especially literature), and a more specific effect on psychiatry. Since Freud we think about ourselves and our behaviour in a different way. Take just three cardinal insights which we owe to Freud: the concept of unconscious motivation, the phenomenon of transference (the projection of positive and negative infantile feelings on to the others) and infantile sexuality. These notions, formulated in the face of bitter opposition, are now part of our culture, and many who have not been near a psychological laboratory are familiar with them. There is unfortunately still mutual incomprehension and suspicion on both sides of the divide. If academics are scornful about 'armchair speculation', psychoanalysts sometimes dismiss experimental psychology as 'behaviourism'. Both accusations are ludicrously unfair. The problem with psychoanalytic theories (as opposed to insights) is that it seems very difficult to determine what observations could falsify them, and hence many would reject them as explanations of mental life. Whether they provide a framework in which to think about abnormal behaviour is a different matter.

So far as chess is concerned, Freudians have gone to extraordinary lengths to convince us that it is a vehicle for parricidal fantasies. The killing of the father in order to possess the mother is assumed to be a ubiquitous fantasy in the male, and the fierce struggle of chess, with all its rich symbolism, is assumed as the battleground on which this universal theme is enacted. The most famous study, 'The Problem of Paul Morphy' by Ernest Jones (1954), started off this line of thought. We are inclined to criticize this account of the motivation behind chess playing, not because it seems implausible, but because (like a perfect jigsaw puzzle) it fits together too well (see Chapter 3, 'Motivation and Talent').

It is unclear what motivating forces compel a person to become a chess player. Certain answers are fairly obvious and need little research – the desire to excel, the tension of an unremitting intellectual struggle, the absorption in a task which precludes the worries of daily life, the allure of self-improvement which in most of us evades a ceiling, and the attraction of constructing a pattern which is often beautiful and always novel in one way or another. All these topics we touch on in the pages which follow.

Chess is the supremely rational game – theoretically the interaction of White and Black force is governed by reason. So would you expect chess players to be rational? Turn to Chapter 8, 'Irrationality', in which we describe the extraordinary beliefs in the paranormal which affected both Karpov and Korchnoi in the World Championship Match at Baguio City in 1978, the importation into the Soviet camp of the parapsychologist, Dr Vladimir Zukhar, and his subsequent removal from a front row in the auditorium. The important thing here is the belief rather than the reality. By virtue of its rationality chess appeals especially to intellectuals. Yet we see here, at the very highest levels, by a kind of ironic compensation, not only a belief in the existence of psychic powers, but an evident attempt to use them to enhance the thought processes of one player, and (possibly) to impair those of the other. In a similar way, some opponents of both Alekhine and of Tal claimed to be under the effects of hypnotic influence. This conviction that some factor other than one's own powers is responsible for bad play is a natural refuge for human vanity – Tartakower coined the aphorism: 'No healthy player has ever lost a game'. By these standards the psychoanalytic interpretations of father murder seem like child's play.

What sort of chess is played by computers (Chapter 6, 'Artificial Stupidity?')? It is acknowledged that today some programs do play reasonable chess, and that they are constantly improving, but they have not yet reached master level – in spite of the early optimistic prophecies of experts in Artificial Intelligence. It seems to us, however, that we should ask a deeper question about the way in which computer chess could illuminate human thinking. The point is not so much whether a computer will ever rival a chess master, but the different ways in which human and machine go about the task. We propose a 'Turing Test' to carry the research forward. In a famous paper 'Computing Machinery and Intelligence', published in the philosophical journal *Mind* in 1950, the mathematician Alan Turing proposed that, if a competent individual were unable to tell the difference between the outputs of a computer and a person, then it is justifiable to conclude that the computer is capable of thinking. Our idea requires a master to try to tell the difference between games played by computers and games played by humans of roughly comparable strength. If a reliable difference were to be detected (especially one at various levels), then we suggest that machine thinking (in chess at least) is qualitatively radically different from human thinking. It would throw little light on the way humans learn to cope with this particular intellectual task.

Other chapters (e.g. Chapter 10, 'The Origins of Skill') are about the social factors which determine an interest in chess – why some countries (e.g. the USSR) and some groups (e.g. the Jews) conspicuously excel; and why other biological groups (e.g. women) tend to lag behind. It is simply an unclear question whether differences like this are innate, or whether they could be demolished through education and a re-structuring of society. In fact, it is not really a terribly interesting question because it is impossible to answer one way or the other. And hence, like all such questions, it is radically infected by propaganda. Still, we make some attempt to deal with it because people like asking these questions.

We find it helpful to think about chess in terms of several dimensions, some of which are independent of each other, and others closely related. 'Talent' and 'Motivation' are clearly independent (or orthogonal) – to be ranked high on one of these dimensions does not imply an equivalent height on the other. Thus, Capablanca could be seen as a player with very high talent but lower motivation. But the dimension of motivation should be sub-divided into two components – 'Competitiveness' and 'Obsession'. The need to win is reflected in competitiveness, and the need to play chess (regardless of the importance of winning) is reflected in obsession. Of course, these two dimensions often occur together in the same person. Alekhine was clearly both obsessed with chess (and valued its artistic qualities), but also possessed a supreme will to win. In contrast, Lasker is a good example of someone who had low obsession – in one period of his career he gave up chess for years – but (like Alekhine) had a very high degree of competitiveness. Many chess addicts – the 'obsessional' players, whose enchantment with the game is never extinguished by defeat – are clearly minimal on competitiveness.

There is a dimension of 'aesthetics', the joy in the beauty of pattern, which seems to be negatively correlated with 'competitiveness'. It seems reasonable to suppose that if you are totally taken up with the wonder of the game, then this is likely to detract from any fighting spirit. In Chapter 2, 'The Nature of Chess', we draw attention to the somewhat heated polemics which Soviet theoreticians have levelled against the competitive element of merely scoring points, at the expense of the artistic (aesthetic) component in the game. The drive to win is assumed by these authorities to be incompatible with the cultural value of chess. Whatever the explanation underlying these attacks, it may be that some people are drawn towards chess because of the opportunity it affords for victory (killing the father?), while others seem attracted by its inherent beauty, and by the way in which every game is a *new* pattern wrought out of vaguely familiar constellations. On the other hand, one might suppose that those who relish beauty, and dislike competition altogether, would be expected to eschew the game and turn their attention to the composition (or solution) of endgame studies, or problems. The bounty of chess caters for many different sorts of taste.

One important question we should like to clarify is the age-old argument about the educational value of chess. Is it, as Bernard Shaw thought, a foolish expedient for making idle people believe they are doing something very clever? In the past chess has almost been regarded magically because of its power to enslave men's minds. The Church has banned it as an activity for priests because of its time-consuming qualities. According to Foxe's *Book of Martyres*, the Czech reformer Jan Huss (1369-1415) confesses the power chess had over his priestly duties. (In contrast to this Christian disapproval on the grounds of absorption it is interesting to note that Ayatollah Khomeini has recently banned chess in Iran because, in the light of the Koran, both games of chance and 'images' (chess pieces) are condemned. But the real reason behind Khomeini's edict is said to be association with the word 'Shah' – Persian for chess.)

One of the earliest attacks in the Christian tradition comes from James I (1566-1625) in *Basilikon Doron* (1599). It epitomizes many of the criticisms:

As for the Chesse, I think it ouer fond, because it is oucrwise and Philosophike a folly: for where all such light playes are ordained to free men's heades for a time from the fashious thoughts on their affairs; it by the contrarie filleth and troubleth men's heades with as many fashious toyes of the playe, as before it was filled with thoughts on his affairs.

It seems unfair today to pick on chess as a waste of time, not only because other activities qualify in the same way, but because a waste of time can also be regarded as a constructive use of our leisure. Other pursuits, which have a lot in common with chess with respect to the tenacious hold they exert on the mind, are computer programming and the writing of philosophical papers. There are many who might dismiss these activities too. Actually, it will be argued that such strenuous diversions are highly beneficial (in moderation) even if they do not necessarily improve our standard of living.

The other side of the argument, however, is equally magical. It has often been claimed in the past, and is still claimed today, that playing chess is of educational benefit for the mind – that it inculcates certain virtues such as foresight, patience, and the ability to accept the consequences of one's decisions. In concrete detail, the rule of not being able to take back a move is assumed to transfer to important decisions of daily life. Benjamin Franklin's *Morals of Chess* (1786) is the best-known example of such romantic claims.

Certainly the theory of chess is highly rational, but it does not follow that its practice will induce rationality, or even the appreciation of rationality in others. Of course, we chess players like to believe that chess will 'help one to concentrate', or instil some other desirable quality. Unfortunately there is little evidence to support these beliefs. Indeed, there is evidence in the psychology of reasoning to suggest that most reasoning in everyday life is context-dependent. In other words, the kind of thinking demanded by chess may be *sui generis*, and unrelated to other activities (see Chapter 5).

But between these two magical views – chess as addiction and chess as morally or intellectually instructive – a real case can be made out for its place in the community. Whether organized in high-level tournaments, or played in the local club, or in moves which arrive through the post on our breakfast table, chess has a splendid escapist value. (The word 'escapist' should not be regarded as pejorative: we all need to escape at times.) Playing a tough game, or solving a

opening, has the power to dispel that pervasive boredom which so
often afflicts us. Dr Tarrasch's famous dictum is often quoted:
'Chess, like love, like music, has the power to make men happy'.
But its context, which provides the reasons, is often left unquoted:

> Chess is a form of intellectual productiveness, therein lies its peculiar
> charm. Intellectual productiveness is one of the greatest joys – if not the
> greatest one – of human existence. It is not everyone who can write a
> play, or build a bridge, or even make a good joke. But in chess everyone
> can, everyone must, be intellectually productive and so can share in this
> select delight.

That just about says it all. We try to fill in some of the details.

2 The Nature of Chess

What is chess? According to the dictionary it is: 'a game for two players with thirty-two pieces or chess men on a chess board chequered with sixty-four squares'. On the other hand, the *Bolshaya Sovetskaya* defines it as: 'an art appearing in the form of a game'. Both definitions are reasonable, but neither helps to elucidate the fact that chess can become an object of unending pursuit, or a highly addictive drug, depending on how you want to look at it. Similarly, one might consider the old question: 'Is chess a game, a science or an art?'. Most chess players are probably too absorbed in the business of mastering chess to worry about such a question. To them the problems raised by chess are more interesting than what appears to be a philosophical problem. In any case, the search for definition is a pseudo-problem which falls into the ancient trap of what Karl Popper (1952) calls 'methodological essentialism' with its roots in the philosophy of Plato and Aristotle. Such a theory assumes that if the *essence* of a thing can be defined then we are well on the way to understanding its nature. The theory is false – in fact, a consideration of the status of chess, and what different people get out of it, will do a great deal to illuminate its falsity.

There is simply little point in asking to what category of human experience chess can be assimilated. But, of course, it is still interesting to enquire about different aspects, or components, of chess which are like, and unlike, those found in other activities. The mistake would be to argue that chess is an art but not a science, or a game but not an art, etc. In any case, the categories are not distinct but frequently overlap. Mathematicians sometimes point out the elegance of their proofs to uncomprehending laymen, and doctors sometimes say, when they don't know what is wrong with you:

'Medicine is really an art, you know'. Thus we shall not attempt to fit chess into any definite slot, but rather try to see how the kind of thinking involved in chess is also involved in other activities. Our question then becomes: 'On what grounds is chess like a game, an art or a science?'. And in attempting to answer it, we shall try to present a broad spectrum of the way in which chess has been conceived.

Chess as a game? This is an obvious candidate about which there can be little dispute. It is not only one of the oldest board games in existence – one estimate gives its birth in India in the fifth or sixth century AD – it is also extremely difficult. (Indeed, it is worth noting, en passant, that exponents of 'artificial intelligence' have argued that if they can get a computer to play chess as well as the best human beings, then they can get it, in principle, to do anything.) This difficulty is reflected in the range of official gradings of skill which have been laid down by FIDE (the official body which governs world chess). However, it has to be admitted that other board games (e.g. backgammon), and card games (e.g. bridge), also allow fine gradations of skill. In fact, the Japanese game of Go probably permits an even finer gradation than chess because scoring in it is almost continuous rather than discrete.

The difficulty of chess has its roots in the mathematical structure of the game. If two very rarely applicable laws of chess governing claims of a draw ('the 50-move rule' and 'the triple occurrence of the same position') are waived, then chess may be considered as infinite as language. On the other hand, even if the occurrence of these remote drawing claims is allowed, then the ordinary mortal can hardly conceive the gigantic number of possibilities which exists in the game which he is playing. It has been estimated that the number of seconds which have elapsed since the Solar System has been in existence is 10^{18}, and that the number of atoms in the Universe is roughly 10^{70}. That is nothing much on chess. Kraitchik (1943) has estimated that the number of possibilities in a 40-move game is 25×10^{115}, and that the number of possible games is roughly 10^{120}. Obviously no human being (or machine) could keep track of possibilities the extent of which makes astronomic distances look miserably dwarfish.

How then does one ever learn to play at all? As everyone knows, the beginner is taught certain maxims, precepts (or technically *heuristics*) of positional play which enable him to cope with apparent disorder, e.g. 'seize open files', 'occupy the 7th rank with a rook', 'avoid isolated pawns', 'put your pawns on opposite coloured squares to those of your bishop' etc etc. However, skill is marked, not by the application of such precepts, but by the correct assessment of their competing claims, or by knowing when to violate them. Consider a concrete case which shows how difficult it is to teach chess. One good positional rule is: 'Never move the same piece twice in the opening'. But in the 1982 BBC World Cup Tournament, grandmaster John Nunn made the same bishop move no less than three times in the opening against the World Champion, Anatoly Karpov – and (as Black too) he drew the game. It is cases like this, perhaps, which make the Soviet school lay such stress on 'concrete analysis of the position' rather than on 'dogma'.

When a higher degree of skill is reached a conscious (verbal) assessment of a position in terms of positional rules is transcended. The master tends to 'zero in' on a position rather than use specific heuristics (see Chapter 5). It has even been argued (Dreyfus, 1972) that the difference between the ability to 'zero in' and sheer reliance on heuristics provides a crux for workers in artificial intelligence who try to write effective programs to enable computers to play master chess. We shall consider this important issue in Chapter 6.

So the difficulty and complexity of the game is one factor which may attract people towards chess. There is not much fun to be gained by doing something which can easily be mastered. But, in addition, many people enjoy chess because they suppose it to be fair. In principle, at least, the outcome of a game depends on error. (Tartakower coined the aphorism: 'The winner made the last blunder but one'.) But it does not depend upon the calculus of probabilities in the way that roulette depends upon it. The opponent's hand lies open on the board. In consequence, the player is inclined to feel (especially when winning) that his intellectual powers are under test. There is, however, an argument for luck in chess which goes something like this. Suppose chess really is too difficult for the human mind to cope with (as might easily be the case according to the available evidence), then all we can do is try to control the pieces as best we can. No matter how well we play, occasionally something unforeseen (or unforeseeable) will spoil things for us. That is just bad luck. Like life, chess can be unfair. An ideal game, one might conjecture, is one where victory can be attributed to skill and defeat to bad luck. Perhaps that is why chess is so popular.

The opposite argument is also compelling. Even if chess is at times unfair in practice, it ought to be fair, or (at any rate) more fair than most things. After all, the play is always susceptible to rational criticism, e.g. 'you lost the game because of weaknesses incurred by moves *x*, *y* and *z*'. This idealized, or perhaps sentimental, view of chess was expressed by Emanuel Lasker (World Champion from 1894 to 1921) in his concept of chess as 'struggle':

> On the chess board lies and hypocrisy do not survive long. The creative combination lays bare the presumption of a lie; the merciless fact, culminating in a checkmate, contradicts the hypocrite. Our little Chess is one of the sanctuaries where this principle of justice has occasionally had to hide to gain sustenance and respite, after the army of mediocrities had driven it from the market-place. And many a man, struck by injustice as, say, Socrates and Shakespeare were struck, has found justice realized on the chess board and has thereby recovered his courage and his vitality to continue to play the game of Life.
>
> *Manual of Chess*, 1932

The psychoanalyst would probably interject here that such a cosy view of chess is a comfortable rationalization which conceals from the player the murderous impulses which motivate his play (see Chapter 3). Still, the idea of chess as justice and order is plausible enough at face value. The international master George Botterill (incidentally a lecturer in philosophy) put it to us (personal communication) like this:

> One of the things that appeals to me about competitive chess (I mean over-the-board chess, though presumably the same goes for corre-spondence chess if there is not too much collusion) is that it is, as games go, *very fair*. There is quite a lot of luck in chess over the short term. But on the whole it tends to cancel out. Certainly chess compares very favourably with all the things that go under the designation 'real life', with all the stacked decks, silver spoons, nepotism, favouritism and disastrous misfortunes that attend. In comparison with the crazy unpredictability and uncontrollability of most of human existence, playing chess (even in a time-scramble!) is like a paradise of rationality. I really do mean that . . .

This is a nice contemporary equivalent of the view expressed by Lasker. (Is it coincidental that both are philosophers?). But if it is this prevailing sense of objectivity, or rationality, or fairness, which induces people to play competitive chess, then what can one say about the importance of winning games, which the psychologist would recognize as the factor of reinforcement? Botterill told us that in his case success was indeed a first stage in the appreciation of chess, but that a second stage was the excitement of competition, and third a feeling for chess as a historical phenomenon with a long and rich tradition. Interestingly enough, grandmaster Michael Stean (personal communication) made the same point: success was important initially, but it is no longer essential later on. (He was unable to identify what it is about chess that maintains his interest.) The relative importance of winning depends on the extent of suffering involved in losing. And here there are what psychologists call 'individual differences' – totally uncompetitive people can lose every game and stay happy. And (as we shall see) there are other branches of chess – the composed ending and the problem – which do not involve competition. The spirit of aggression, which characterizes chess as a game, does not seem to be sufficient to account for the spell which it exerts over its followers. Its strong aesthetic appeal makes chess a worthy candidate as an art.

Although Réti was trained as a mathematician he wrote like a poet: 'A hundred years ago chess was no doubt only a game, but he who has felt, for example, the deep sense of devotion that pervades Rubinstein's games knows that we find there a new and ever progressing art' (*Modern Ideas in Chess*, 1923). What does it mean – 'deep sense of devotion' and 'ever progressing art'? At least part of what it means is that chess affords a unique medium of self-expression to those who practise it, and that changes in chess theory are paralleled by movements in the arts. Indeed, Réti draws an analogy between the development of abstract art, e.g. cubism, in the 1920s, and the rise of the 'hypermodern school' in chess. It is also fairly well known that devotion to chess can become obsessive, and starvation from it can lead to withdrawal symptoms – even Botvinnik in his autobiography (1981) refers to his 'chess hunger'. In ancient India men are said to have abandoned their wives for it, and (more recently) Marcel Duchamp's wife secretly glued down the pieces on his chess board during their honeymoon (Cockburn, 1975). Thus, quite aside from any competitive element, chess can inspire devotion as a vehicle of self-expression; it produces aesthetic effects, and changes in its theory resemble those in the arts. But in a different sense it may qualify as an art. The master's cognitive activity, which allows him to find the best move, is not wholly reducible to rational (scientific) principles. We do not wish to pre-empt our discussion of this complex issue, with which we are concerned in Chapter 5, but it is worth pointing out here that the late Gerald Abrahams (*The Chess Mind*, 1951) argued persuasively that the most important mental activity in chess is *vision* – 'the unforced intuition of possibilities by the mind's eye'. In a single sentence, and most probably without knowing any of the intensive psychological experimentation, Abrahams summed up the research which we shall describe subsequently: 'Seeing the idea precedes the logical argument'. This capacity for vision, whatever one means precisely by that term, obviously reinforces the notion of chess as an art because it is not a matter of exact calculations.

If it is an art then it would seem to follow that it is also a creative activity. As we shall see, the Soviets almost seem to drive a wedge between 'creative chess' (a good thing) and merely 'competitive chess' (a bad thing). On the other hand, some authorities argue that there is very little genuine creativity in chess, and that the thinking engaged in it is mainly interpretative – the recognition and interpretation of concepts rather than the creation of ideas. In fact, the difference between the two views here is terminological and clouded by the notoriously vague word 'creative', with its honorific connotations. Psychologists have had a difficult time in establishing the criteria for the creative act – a difficulty which is mirrored by the concept of 'intelligence'. A great deal of interesting research was conducted, mainly in the United States in the 1950s and 1960s, on creative individuals and creative achievements, but the whole topic is now very unfashionable, probably because of methodological difficulties in separating 'creativity' and 'intelligence', and the rise of different kinds of problem. 'Creativity' has become too much of an umbrella term covering too many different kinds of behaviour. In one sense, it is applied to startling and novel achievements in the arts and sciences, when a product deviates sharply from the tradition of work in the field. Perhaps the psychologist Jerome Bruner's (1961) definition of a creative act is the best one for creativity in this narrow sense: a creative product is marked by 'effective surprise'. It is not enough for it to be merely effective, and it is not enough for it to be merely surprising – it has to be both. It is worth mentioning that part of the difficulty with such a definition, and with most of the others that have been proposed, is that one can only apply it *after* the act has been performed, and probably only after a considerable time has elapsed – for only then can one determine whether the work in question has been influential for others in the field. (All the same, an interest in this kind of creativity should emphatically not be dismissed because of the conceptual and methodological snags which surround its investigation.) On the other hand, the utterance of a grammatical sentence has been said by Chomsky (1957) to be creative because it may put together elements (governed by rules) in a totally novel, 'generative', way. And some would like to call the behaviour of lower organisms creative. The trouble here is that in this weaker sense the term 'creative' can be stretched to cover every kind of behaviour, or mental activity, which cannot be explained by invoking principles of rote learning.

Obviously, chess can be considered creative in this weaker sense. Indeed, there is a nice analogy between contemporary (transformationalist) concepts of language, i.e. potentially infinite output governed by a small number of fixed rules, and chess. But even in the strong sense of the word a great deal of chess surely qualifies for creative achievement in Bruner's idea of 'effective surprise'. On what evidence does this claim rest? At a basic level, the notion of an 'innovation', or 'discovery', in the theory of a particular opening (which often causes text books to be revised) would seem to constitute an instance of creative thought characterized by effective surprise. At a more orchestrated level the emergence of new schools, notably the hypermodern school, with its somewhat paradoxical and outrageous slogans ('Not to build up but to obstruct a position', 'After 1 e2-e4 White's game is in its last throes') parallels (as we pointed out previously) the shocking tenets of Dada and other 'modernistic' art movements. Such schools in chess do seem to constrain the development of chess thinking in ways which (at the time) are novel. But perhaps the most striking, and unequivocal, examples of creativity in chess can be found in the world of chess problems. One such problem – the 'Indian problem' – is the most famous example; it has inspired books devoted to its study. The problem, composed by the Rev. H.A.Loveday (under a pseudonym) was published in *The Chess Player's Chronicle* in 1845 (see diagram).

In an interesting way its construction was highly inaccurate, but the idea behind it, involving what is known as 'critical play', was revolutionary. At that time it was enormously difficult to solve. H.Weenink (1926) pointed out in *The Chess Problem*: 'Loveday . . . was the first to demonstrate difficulty of solution resulting from the application of a preconceived strategic sequence as rigorously interdependent as the elements of a syllogism . . .'. Thus a totally new

H.A.LOVEDAY *Chess Player's Chronicle* February 1845
Mate in 4
The Original 'Indian Problem'

Solution: **1 ♔b1 (or 1 ♖d8 or 1 ♗h1) 1 ... b4 2 ♗c1! b5 3 ♖d2!
♔f4 4 ♖d4 mate**

idea was exemplified (probably by chance) on the chess board by a
clergyman in Bombay who contributed it anonymously to a chess
magazine, with the result that chess problemists started thinking in a
different way. This reads like the 'paradigm case' of creativity in
chess. But, of course, moments like this are infrequent. A reasonable
verdict would be that chess is always creative in the weak sense of the
term (novelty of production), and sometimes creative in the strong
sense of the term (effective surprise).

At any rate, exponents of the Soviet School wax most eloquent
about the critical importance of creativity in chess. Thus ex-World
Champion Smyslov (1958) describes how chess first influenced him:
'I saw in chess an interesting realm of creative ideas, based on the
opposing conception of two players, who in the course of a tense
struggle strive to create a work of art.' And, rather amusingly, Tal
(Soltis, 1976) characterizes the style of a young grandmaster as
having 'no creative handwriting'. What is most interesting, however,
is the attempt to differentiate between creative and competitive
features of the play. The late Alexander Kotov, a sort of official
spokesman of the Soviet School, in his book *Train Like a Grandmaster*
(1981), castigates a 'tribe' of grandmasters and masters who fail to
conform to his ideals:

Our beloved art is becoming unfortunately a mere 'arithmetical game',
not just in the reckoning up of full and half points, but in its very essence

– in the process of thinking about moves. This arithmetic is clearly killing creativity and that leads to sad results. Only a few grandmasters have been able to avoid this risky trend, and they find their reward in the achievement of the highest results, in becoming world champions and challengers for this title. The majority, alas, including many young grandmasters, have completely rejected the analytical approach. For this they are being punished by chess, the punishment being their gradual transformation into hacks, destroying all the bright prospects due to their natural talent.

It is suggested, by way of remedy, that the 'liquidation of the arithmetical deviation is the social duty of the players themselves'. Particularly revealing is the early comment by Kotov and Yudovich (1958) on Petrosian:

Latterly, however, a tendency to evade complications and to try to win games by technical superiority has become apparent; colourless draws have appeared in his tournament play. It is to be hoped that an exacting attitude towards himself plus the young grandmaster's modesty and industry will enable him to display his chess talents more strikingly than ever before and to give us many new examples of chess virtuosity.

Five years later, having perfected colourless play, Petrosian won the World Championship.

We might ask where we have heard this unctuous and self-righteous tone before. Surely in the typical prep school end-of-term reports, e.g. 'if only he would try harder and concentrate on his lessons he would be capable of the highest achievements'.

The notion of chess as creative, rather than competitive, is evidently firmly established in the highest echelons of Soviet chess circles. A recent book by grandmaster David Bronstein and G.Smolyan, *Chess in the Eighties* (1982), expresses concern (among other issues) about the 'sport-orientated' nature of chess, in which the result is all-important, to the detriment of chess as an art form. One might imagine the Soviets were losing their supremacy and looking around for compensating features. What is the cause of the rather strange differentiation between two styles of playing, and the stridency with which it is sometimes voiced? The vehement style of writing, with its denunciations of the deviant, is of course consistent with the Marxist-Leninist rhetoric – recall the style of Lenin himself. One might have supposed, however, that the chess esteem of a nation *would* have been reflected in a measure of its success. Surely a country whose team in the Olympiad played elegant chess, but whose score gave it bottom place, would not acquire much esteem. The answer may be that the stress on artistry (and presumably aesthetic satisfaction) is deemed necessary to attract beginners (and youth generally) towards a pursuit which specifically enjoins detachment from the external world. In the words of Alekhine (Kotov, 1975): 'During a chess competition a chess master should be a combination of a beast of prey and a monk'. Presumably the beast of prey aspect is supposed to take second place to the monk.

Nobody would really deny these two aspects in chess, but whether they can be separated and evaluated differently is quite another matter. If the beauty of the game as art were a primary motivator, one would be content, indeed fulfilled, by losing a beautiful game. But most of us would admit (if we were honest) that the ultimate misery in chess is to lose a brilliancy prize. It is a common, though sad, occurrence for a player to select a miserable way to lose just to deny the opponent the satisfaction of creating a work of art. The beauty of the game seems to be part of the victor's spoils. In fact, it could be argued that it is not the game of chess, which does involve competition, but its two other major branches which provide a medium for aesthetic expression.

The composed endgame (or study) is a bridge between the game and the totally different world of the problem. It maintains all the conventions of the game, and because the composer is able to control both sides it affords the greatest scope for the realization, in ideal form, of combinative ideas that could occur (or have occurred) in a game. Some of the most distinguished grandmasters of the game, e.g. Réti and Botvinnik, have been first-class composers of studies. And in both cases they have used their own games as stimulus material. Indeed, Golombek relates in his introduction to *Modern Ideas in Chess* (1923) that Réti became so captivated by an idea during the playing of a tournament game that he not only lost that particular game (which was easily won for him), but spent all night working on the study with the consequence that he lost the following game – and the tournament – as well. The artistic lure of expressing an idea in perfect form here overcame any competitive drive. The ideas of an opponent do not come in to spoil the picture. As Alekhine (Kotov, 1975) put it: 'The ideas and fantasy of someone else, which are all too often mediocre, are eliminated'. (Incidentally, by far the best introduction to the beauties of studies is John Roycroft's *Test Tube Chess*, 1972.)

The chess problem is altogether more remote, and it is certainly true that its greatest exponents are seldom (or never) to be found among the grandmasters of the game. Most chess players, probably wrongly, remain indifferent to the problem world because the stipulation of mate in a given number of moves entails positions which seem fantastic to the player. Even within the problem world certain recent developments connected with the formal property of problems have caused a heated controversy among problemists. But probably what disturbs the player is that nearly all problems are overwhelming wins for White. It is reasonable to conjecture, not that the typical chess player fails to understand that the aims of the problem are totally different to those of the game, but that the positions demanding solution do not arouse the chess knowledge which is part of the player's intellectual equipment (see Chapter 5). At one level he may appreciate the aphorism of the great mathematician G.H.Hardy: 'A chess problem is an exercise in pure mathematics'. But at a deeper level, because of his stored knowledge of what goes on in the game, the problem with its conventions is not readily assimilated to this knowledge. It is little wonder that the language used for discussing problems is totally different from that used to discuss the game. The late problemist Brian Harley (1931) imagines a fellow problemist, Barry Andrade, accosting a stranger in the Gambit Restaurant up for the day from the country for a quiet game of chess. 'Now, here is a Lateral Anti-Bristol with a two-spot diagonal Wurzburg Plachutta. Do you think a third spot could be worked in? Or don't you?' Such technicalities, which have their counterpart in the language of the game, describe the mechanism of problems. There cannot be a specialized language to describe the powerful aesthetic effects which are felt by both the composer and the solver. In an eloquent passage, Nabokov has tried to capture the emotions of the composer when an idea for a problem occurs. He stresses the spontaneity of the occurrence and the deep satisfaction involved in working it out – phenomena which are typical of the process of discovery in both the arts and the sciences. Contrary to what many people suppose, original ideas come when they are least expected. It is worth pointing out that there is sometimes a special sort of satisfaction to be gained from problems and studies – not just an aesthetic response to elegance, but an appreciation of *wit*. In fact, it is almost impossible not to be amused by working through the solution of some problems. This amusement seems to derive from the completely unexpected way in which the White and Black forces interact – an interaction more dramatic (and subtle) than the sacrificial combinations which may occur in the game. The problems of the great American 'Puzzle-King' Sam Loyd (1841-1911) are especially distinguished in this way. One of his most famous problems – 'The Lovechase' (technically analysed as 'Black Invalidation, White Non-Provision') shows how a White queen must tread exactly to track the movements of a Black bishop (see diagram).

S.LOYD *Leipziger Illustrierte Zeitung* 1869
Mate in 3
'The Lovechase'
(Black Invalidation, White Non-Provision)

Solution: 1 ♕f1 ♗b2 2 ♕b1 g6 3 ♕xb2 mate
1 ♕f1 ♗c3/d4 2 ♕d3 g6 3 ♕xc3/d4 mate
1 ♕f1 ♗e5/f6 2 ♕f5 g6 3 ♕xe5/f6 mate
1 ♕f1 g3 2 ♘g6+ hg 3 ♕h3 mate

Since problems, arguably the most artistic form of chess, can also be analysed in a formal language, a claim might be strongly made that every branch of chess (game, study, problem) is basically science rather than art. The theory of the game, especially the opening but also the middle game and ending, is in a constant state of development as new ideas are tried out in important tournaments and matches. And just like the situation in scientific research, where papers in learned journals modify existing knowledge, hypotheses about innovations in chess are subjected to experimental verification (or falsification) during play or in analysis. A couple of examples. The American grandmaster Frank Marshall analysed a variation of the Ruy Lopez (the Marshall Attack) over a period of years, holding it in reserve until he had an opportunity to encounter Capablanca

(New York, 1918). Marshall lost the justly celebrated game, but the attack which he invented lived on, and is still a topic of theoretical debate. An even more striking case of preparation occurred in the 1945 Radio Match between the USA and the USSR. After Smyslov's 23rd move the American Team Captain radioed for the time consumed by Smyslov. The American, Reshevsky, who had taken one hour and a half, discovered that his opponent Smyslov had taken exactly *one minute*. He was up against a prepared variation. The entire analysis, up to the 23rd move at least, had been published (unbeknown to the Americans) in the June 1945 issue of *Shakhmaty v SSSR*.

Intensive analytical work is often collaborative in the USSR especially. This, again, is similar to scientific research. Just as scientists have their research assistants, so do grandmasters have their trainers or seconds. An amusing incident connected with collaboration is recounted by Botvinnik in his autobiography (*Achieving the Aim*, 1981) about a game he played in the 1954 Olympiad at Amsterdam:

> A dramatic situation arose in my game with Unzicker. An opening experiment in the French Defence led to a lost position. The whole game I hung on by my finger tips. We adjourned in a rook endgame in which, according to the general opinion of experts, it was time to resign.
>
> We had to work at it. First of all Boleslavsky helped, but soon his head started drooping and he went off to sleep. He was replaced by Flohr, who put up a good show. When I woke him up he gave good advice. At 2 am I sent him off to rest with the warning that at 8 am he should come back and assess the results of his analysis.
>
> Flohr turned up at 8 and found two ways to win [for Unzicker]; one of them I refuted (or so it seemed to me). On the whole this was quite good. Unzicker might not notice these finesses! [The game was drawn]

Consider one more respect in which the practice of chess resembles the practice of science. In both there is an accepted body of knowledge which gradually accumulates – 'the book' in chess and 'the literature' in science. In both the vast majority of practical work is conventional and stereotyped. In chess the same opening systems are slavishly imitated, and in science the same experimental designs (and 'paradigms') dominate the journals. In both the plodding researchers extend theory by assuming existing knowledge, exploring the boundaries, while the genuine innovators correct, or change, the accepted knowledge. The analogy between chess and science, rather than between chess and art, would seem to be conclusively

established by this account of the Soviet School (written by
Botvinnik in 1951):

> What are the principles of our school? First and foremost I must
> mention our scientific approach to chess. This implies a realistic attitude
> to the game and a critical approach towards one's own creative work ...
> And so Soviet masters are continually seeking something new,
> continually exploring new roads in the realm of chess theory and
> practice. For instance, certain masters of days past played the same
> opening year after year; but we approach the problem differently. When
> we study some opening system, when we evolve a 'new production
> technique', we make use of the system only so long as it brings advantage,
> and then we scrap it and renew the search for a fresh 'weapon'.

But such a view may be controversial even within the USSR.
Bronstein thought that Botvinnik's scientific approach took the joy
out of the game. He later said that his match with Botvinnik in 1951
was just an attempt to prove that chess could still be played
intuitively, and without the clinical precision Botvinnik tried to
demonstrate. If you like, the 1951 World Championship was played
to determine whether chess is science or art. The final score was 12:12.

In any case, despite what Botvinnik says about the characteristics
of the Soviet School, it would be quite wrong to suppose that he
considers chess to be a science. Indeed, in the early 1960s he
explicitly denied it could be a science because, according to Marxism,
science studies the laws of nature, society or thought. And, instead, in
an interesting passage, he comes down firmly in favour of chess as an
art in which the connoisseur appreciates the creative, logical side of
human thought, and receives an impression of human thinking in the
form of specific artistic chess images. 'Logic studies the laws of
thinking, but chess in the form of artistic images reflects, as an art,
the logical side of thought ...' All this is taken from that informative
and scholarly book by D.J.Richards, *Soviet Chess* (1965).

We seem to have come round in a circle to the point made at
the beginning of this chapter. The search for definitions is unfruitful.
We can read into chess anything we please to suit our individual
temperaments or needs. Let Stefan Zweig, in his short story *The Royal
Game* (1945), have the last word:

> But is it not an offensively narrow construction to call chess a game? Is it
> not a science, a technique, an art, that sways among these categories as
> Mahomet's coffin does between heaven and earth, at once a union of all

contradictory concepts: primeval yet ever new; mechanical in operation yet effective only through the imagination; bounded in geometric space though boundless in its combinations; ever developing yet sterile; thought that leads to nothing; mathematics that produce no results; art without works; architecture without substance, and nevertheless, as proved by evidence, more lasting in its being and presence than all books and achievements; the only game that belongs to all people and all ages; of which none knows the divinity that bestowed it on the world, to slay boredom, to sharpen the senses, to exhilarate the spirit. One searches for its beginning and for its end. Children can learn its simple rules, duffers succumb to its temptation, yet within this immutable tight square it creates a particular species of master not to be compared with any other – persons destined for chess alone, specific geniuses in whom vision, patience and technique are operative through a distribution no less precisely ordained than in mathematicians, poets, composers, but merely united on a different level.

3 Motivation and Talent

In the previous chapter we tried to convey something of the richness of chess and the different ways in which it has been conceived. Now we ask a more basic and down-to-earth question: 'why do people play chess, or go to the bother of making up chess compositions?'. Why do they seek the apparent (and time-consuming) torture of creating and solving puzzles which have no use beyond themselves? One might say that the answers would be as banal as the questions. They enjoy it. Just as some individuals thrive on the physical exertion involved in sport, some on the suicidal thrills involved in driving motor cars at ridiculous speeds, so there are particular kinds of people who seek the more cerebral satisfactions involved in chess. But do we know anything else about this class of individuals? The answer to this question is not at all clear, and is suffused with speculation. And part of the reason for this (as we shall see in Chapter 5) is that psychologists have been mainly concerned with understanding chess skill, where they have made a considerable advance in existing knowledge, rather than with problems of motivation, or the relation of chess talent to other kinds of mental capacity. There is a hiatus between the fashionable cognitive research on chess skill, which now owes a considerable debt to theorizing in terms of computer programs, and motivational factors which incline a person to exercise these skills in the first place. What could it mean to ask how the famous 'will to win' could be represented in a computer program? It is ironic that the layman would almost certainly call this 'psychology', while academic psychologists tend increasingly to devote themselves to questions which exclude the operation of emotional, or affective, factors. It is still worth pointing out that such factors may dominate the life of the chess player, whether they are sublimations of aggressive impulses or defences against boredom and ennui. In this connection it is of interest to note that an unpublished result of Hartston, using a projective test designed to elicit information on a subject's 'construct system' (i.e. roughly his system of values), showed that chess players attach considerably more importance to qualities of drive and determination than do comparable groups of non-players. Thus the sheer obligation to win in chess may reflect a more general character trait.

One might start a rather speculative enquiry about chess talent by postulating two extreme ideas in order to see how well the evidence fits them. On the one hand, some individuals are born with a specific chess talent (almost a 'chess gene') which only awaits a minimum of experience to be made manifest; on the other hand, the mind is a *tabula rasa* without the impress of any latent potentiality for chess, and hence the experience of playing it is sufficient to account for proficiency. A dichotomy of this kind corresponds to rationalist and empiricist theories of language development. So far as chess is concerned, the empiricist theory, which rests entirely on the role of experience, seems to us false. We are all familiar with people who are addicted to chess without significantly improving their performance. Nobody could accuse them of lack of practice. Of course, it is just possible that such players are deficient in effort ('weakness of will'?) rather than knowledge, and this suggests a theoretical distinction between the factors predisposing someone towards chess and the factors which contribute towards success in it. Such a distinction would account (at one extreme) for those obsessionally bad players who appear to need chess, and (at the other extreme) for those great masters, such as Lasker, Capablanca and Hübner, who appear to be quite content without playing at all over periods of time. This theoretical distinction, however, is not only difficult to verify, but also complicates the elegance of the sharp division which we are attempting to draw. The extreme version of the empiricist theory – only experience is necessary to excel – merely mirrors the optimistic (and irritating) popular appeal that anyone can do anything if only they set about it in the right way. A common manifestation of it is often heard in relation to painting: 'Of course, you could draw if only you were to *look*'. An even more foolhardy version assumes that any mathematician could become an Einstein.

The extreme version of the rationalist view ('chess talent is inborn') is somewhat implausible, but a modified view is much more plausible

– individuals who take to chess do so by virtue of some kind of innate predisposition which might be manifest in other activities. The evidence is quite compelling that experience alone is not sufficient to account for certain well known extraordinary cases of precocious talent. Morphy learned the moves at ten, and was one of the strongest amateurs of his town within two years. At twenty he won the First American Championship and the next year travelled to Europe where he defeated all the world's leading masters, including Anderssen. Capablanca learned the moves at five, and won the championship of Cuba at twelve. Fischer was awarded the grandmaster title at sixteen, and so on.

Of special interest is the case of the American grandmaster Samuel Reshevsky, a contender for the world title in 1948, because his powers were investigated by a psychologist. Franziska Baumgarten (1939) subjected him to a series of psychological tests when he was eight-and-a-half, about the time when he had been giving simultaneous exhibitions throughout Europe and the United States. Apparently the usual devices for gaining rapport with the interviewer (chocolates, toys etc) were useless. The only effective aid was a stop-watch. His verbal intelligence, for a boy of that age, was low – he failed to recognize pictures of a lion, a monkey, a tiger and a camel. A fox (or wolf) he called a dog, and a bat he called a bird. He did not know the names of the elementary colours, and (interestingly) he was below standard in arithmetic for his age. However, as Reuben Fine (1967) has pointed out, these particular tests suffer from a methodological weakness; they fail to take into account Reshevsky's lack of formal education, and that his native tongue was Polish. The results of the remaining tests which were administered appear to be more valid: they revealed a marked superiority rather than a deficit. On tests of spatial visualisation, requiring (for instance) the combination of a number of irregular forms to produce a regular form, he did very well indeed. He solved one such problem which had been beyond all other children in that age group. Similarly, his memory for forms proved to be a better performance than had ever been previously obtained, even on adults. After inspecting forty figures for four minutes, he was able to restate them without a single error in the order in which they had been shown. In addition to these fairly specific cognitive powers, his personality was assessed as highly self-reliant, a trait which the investigator observed is marked in gifted children. On being asked what he would do if the curtains were to catch fire, he replied: 'Get a bucket of water and throw it on the flames'. 'But why not call the fire brigade?'. 'I want to see to it myself'.

All these cases of early giftedness for chess, combined, at least for Reshevsky, with evident spatial intelligence, support the idea of an innate predisposition. (It is worth pointing out, incidentally, that the case of Sultan Khan suggests an extraordinary unique talent which was not associated with any other accomplishment. A serf on an Indian estate, he not only defeated Capablanca in one memorable game but won the British Championship in 1929, 1932 and 1933. He could neither read nor write.)

But it also seems to be true that considerable experience of chess, and indeed hard work, is necessary in order to attain mastership. Morphy played hundreds of games in occasional contests in his teens. Simon and Chase (1973), whose research on chess skill we shall survey in Chapter 5, have put it like this:

> First, there are no instant experts in chess – certainly no instant masters or grandmasters. There appears not to be on record any case (including Bobby Fischer) where a person has reached grandmaster level with less than about a decade's intense preoccupation with the game. We would estimate, very roughly, that a master has spent perhaps 10,000 to 50,000 hours staring at chess positions . . . For the master, these times are comparable to the times that highly literate people have spent in reading by the time they reach adulthood.

There is ample evidence, too, that dedication to theoretical aspects of chess is important in order to keep abreast with current knowledge. For example, one section of that wonderful book *Grandmaster Preparation* (1981) by Lev Polugayevsky, entitled 'The Birth of a Variation', recounts, in 83 packed pages, the author's 21-year experience of testing and analysing the Polugayevsky Variation of the Sicilian Defence. It moves from an initial cynicism about the value of the variation to a dramatic enlightenment in which everything was seen in a new and different aspect. (Such a total transformation of a problem is typical, incidentally, of conceptual crises in scientific research.) Hard work, experience, practice – we might say that these things are necessary in order to excel. But at the same time we might suppose that they are not sufficient. Provisionally, we might therefore suggest the hypothesis that, without some kind of innate talent, possibly connected with spatial intelligence, sheer indulgence and application is unlikely to create mastership.

It was just this spatial ability, which we saw was so marked in the psychological investigation of the young Reshevsky, which attracted Alfred Binet (the inventor of intelligence tests) to conduct the first psychological investigation of chess playing in 1893. His report, "Les Grandes Mémories: Résumé d'une Enquête sur les Joueurs d'Echecs", is available in translation (1966). Influenced to a large extent by the feat of blindfold chess – Philidor's achievement of playing two games simultaneously blindfold had been hailed as the most impressive feat of the human mind ever – Binet supposed that he was investigating the 'visualisation' and 'memory' of the chess player. It would be more accurate today to say that he was really concerned with 'representation', a fashionable topic in contemporary cognitive psychology concerned with the manner in which events are encoded mentally so that they can be symbolically manipulated. Instead of objective tests, Binet used questionnaires ('distributed throughout the four corners of the chess world') and direct interviewing. Whatever the limitations of such techniques with respect to explanations, he was able to elicit most interesting introspective material from his respondents. The main result of the survey was that strength in play is positively related to an increasing freedom from the visual image of the board and men. A first group, consisting of what he called 'plain amateurs', imagine the chessboard exactly as if they were looking at it attentively – 'a veritable photograph in which the board appears clearly with its black and white squares, and all the pieces are present in colour and with their characteristic shapes'. In an intermediate group of players the mental image is not as clear as it would be in actual vision. At the highest level the mental images of the master are 'stripped of all material and concrete baggage'. There seems to be a considerable unanimity about the central features of these accounts, and a single extended quote, from Tarrasch, is cited as typical:

> A novice playing at the board sees only the details of the chessboard and the particular form of the chessmen because he cannot grasp their intrinsic significance. Conversely, the player absorbed in the strategy of the game does not see a piece of wood with a horse's head, but the course prescribed for the knight, that is worth approximately three pawns, that is perhaps at the moment badly placed at the edge of the board, or about to wage a decisive attack, or in danger of being nailed down by the adversary, etc. In other words, he does not see a wooden figure; he is oblivious to its material aspects, he perceives the significance of the

piece as a knight . . . . The player concentrates his effort and attention to the exclusion of everything else . . . . Though his gaze may rest mechanically on some external details, he is completely unaware of their nature . . . . I could not say whether cardboard or wooden chessboards were used during the tournament in Dresden in 1892; even if someone had asked me as soon as I left the table on what kind of board the last game had been played, I would not have known the answer. Yet I still know by heart nearly all the games I played there . . . . The white queen of the set I use at home has lost her head, and from time to time my wife glues it on with sealing wax. After a game I wouldn't venture to say whether I had played with a complete or headless queen.

Tarrasch's remarks, as we would expect of a good physician, are a good description of the way in which proficiency, or connoisseurship, transforms perception. One of us (WRH) reports a similar experience when playing with non-standard chessmen. At the start of the game there is a feeling of unfamiliarity and confusion, but as soon as play starts the shape of the men becomes totally ignored and irrelevant to the perception of the position. Such an experience seems to be normal among good players. A similar kind of thing happens in a completely tacit way in the perception of art: a Picasso will look very different to an expert compared with someone ignorant of abstract art. Steinitz once put it more bluntly: 'Have you ever seen a monkey examining a watch?'. It is the effortless nature of such tacit discrimination which may seem surprising to the layman. 'Hum, they are good players', said Reuben Fine (de Groot, 1965) while strolling past a chess cafe in Amsterdam without slowing his pace. It is, of course, impossible to test the veracity, or the motivation, for this kind of remark. But it is, at least, entirely compatible with what we know about chess skill (see Chapter 5).

As we have pointed out, Binet's pioneering research suffers from the limitations of introspection (or retrospection) which, as every psychologist knows, is an inadequate way of understanding mental skill. Not only is it subject to unconscious distortion, but it is a poor instrument for revealing all that one knows. In a general way, one might say that one knows much more than one can tell. Verbal, conscious, expression captures only a fragment of mental capacity.

In 1927 a group of Soviet psychologists, Djakow, Rudik and Petrovsky, subjected twelve grandmasters, who had competed in the Moscow (1925) International Tournament, to a series of psychometric tests. The investigation aimed to study 'all the essential aspects of the mental activity of the chess player, as they have been sufficiently described in the literature'. In fact, it was mainly confined to psychometric tests of memory. The results showed that the grandmasters were vastly superior to the control subjects (not further specified) in all tasks relating to chess, but in other tasks the superiority was maintained in only two tests – the ability to pay attention to different things simultaneously (Aufmerksamkeits-verteilung), and a test of abstract thinking. This is rather what we would be inclined to expect from research conducted at a later date – the powers exhibited in chess proficiency may be restricted to the medium of chess (see Chapter 5).

The famous (or infamous) Rorschach Test ('Ink Blot Test') of personality was also administered. For some reason or other, the Russian experimenters did not comment on these results, but Fine (1967) does do so. They suggested that the 'modal personality' of a strong chess player is that of a constricted, 'coarted individual' (no colour and no movement). Rorschach (1932) explains further what is meant by this:

> The coarted type [is] characterized by the extreme emphasis on those tendencies which can be heightened by the application of conscious attention. The coarted and the coartive is in the first place one who is logically disciplined. This is attained, however, by an atrophy of the introversive and extratensive tendencies: by a sacrifice of his capacity for experience.

Stripped of jargon this seems to mean that chess players are capable of clear thinking and their dedication to this mode of expression leaves them uninterested in anything else. In any case, there is a whiff of circularity about this kind of finding. Does one need a predisposition to be logically disciplined in order to be good at chess, or does the study of chess teach one to be logically disciplined? Whatever the causal direction, the finding is hardly surprising. Today the Rorschach Test is considered to be an invalid and unreliable test of personality.

It is all too easy to criticize research carried out in previous decades on the ground that it is in some way methodologically flawed. Psychologists, with their swiftly changing paradigms, like to indulge in this game. Somebody once remarked that they have never yet read a paper (in an official capacity) that was not methodologically flawed. How does this apply to previous research on chess? Binet's introspective study is flawed in its approach, and yet it clearly delineated (in rather a nice way) some basic facts about chess perception. Baumgarten's assessment of Reshevsky provided a possibly faulty picture of his intelligence, but some 'hard data' on the idiosyncratic way in which his mind excelled. Finally, the tests carried out by Djakow, Rudik and Petrovsky, although motivated by a discredited 'faculty psychology', in which the mind is assumed to consist of separate faculties, at least made the important suggestion that the memory of the chess player is largely confined to chess.

So far, it will not have escaped notice that the question posed at the beginning of this chapter, about why people play chess, has been conspicuously unanswered. We have been wholly concerned with talent to the exclusion of motivation. As we hinted at the beginning, there may not be specific factors which govern chess addiction. On the other hand, psychoanalysts think otherwise. It is worth saying a few things in general about psychoanalytic theory. Quite apart from the efficacy of the method as a form of treatment, the theory itself, based on Freud's clinical observations, is usually regarded as disreputable in Departments of Psychology because of its lack of scientific rigour. Indeed, it is sometimes dismissed with emotion, perhaps because its influence on culture has been much greater than that of any theory dreamed up in the academic Psychological Laboratory. This is not to deny that the theory is open to criticism. We shall suggest that its application to chess has been uncritical and (possibly) devoid of empirical content. Like the astrologer's horoscope, some of its claims fit so well that we might be inclined to acclaim its vacuous truth with a rapturous welcome. On the other hand, the fervour with which some critics dismiss it suggests that it may contain the seeds of truth. The difficulty, of course, lies in testing the theory. At the core of this difficulty is the use of discursive language, more like that used in theology than in the physical, or social, sciences with their stress on quantification. But this is not the place to discuss the status of the theory in general. We are concerned with its application.

The Problem of Paul Morphy (1954), by Ernest Jones (the official biographer of Freud and a keen amateur chess player) set the fashion. Jones was a medical analyst, and much of the paper is concerned with the aetiology of the paranoid psychosis to which Morphy finally succumbed. But the paper also suggests that the allure of the game is not a mere outlet for aggressive impulses. It is an unconscious vehicle for the grimmer enactment in fantasy of father-murder (parricide). Its mathematical structure, in addition, allows for the expression of anal-sadistic drives which adapts it so perfectly to the homosexual and antagonistic aspects of the father-son struggle. The paper is a masterpiece in its literary quality and scholarship. If the major premise is granted, then everything follows with a wonderful feeling of inevitability. The snag is that, if a particular kind of motivation can only be verified, not through patient clinical observation, but through biographical data, then it is easy to be struck by the facts which confirm it. The whole jigsaw puzzle of Morphy's life – his glorious domination of Europe at the age of twenty, his fruitless negotiations with the elderly and irascible Staunton, right down to his rejection by a Louisiana girl as a mere chess player – all fall into the Freudian matrix just a little too neatly. It is the beguiling aptness of the interpretation which should give us pause for thought. As Sir Karl Popper has made clear in a number of writings (e.g. 1959), it is not so much plausibility as implausibility which is the hallmark of a scientific theory. If parricide were the unique unconscious motivation of dedicated chess playing, then it would be fair to ask for further evidence. An empirical test does suggest itself. A reasonable derivation of the Freudian theory would be that a strong chess player would lose interest in the game (or fall off in playing strength) after his father had died. What is the motivation of fantasy parricide when there is no father left to kill? If this were found to be true, in a properly conducted scientific investigation with adequate controls, then psychoanalysts would (presumably) be justifiably jubilant. On the other hand, if this prediction were not confirmed, then they could equally justifiably point out that it is not the *actual* father who is critically important to sustain the fantasies, but the image of the father, internalized and without relevance to a living person. This is what might be meant by Popper's criticism of psychoanalysis as untestable, and hence lacking scientific status.

Apart from this rather obvious criticism of applied psychoanalytic theory, one might query more specifically the singling out of chess as the parricide vehicle, and this will be even more relevant to Reuben Fine's interpretations which we shall consider shortly. It seems to be assumed that there is a symbolic identity between the King and the father, and between the Queen and the mother. From this it would appear to follow that if the sex of these pieces were to be transposed, then the psychological profiles of successful players would be totally altered. This seems somewhat unlikely. Then again, why is no case made for the father-loving misogynist grandmaster who lovingly cares for his *own* King and fights against the influence of the enemy Queen. And isn't it a good thing to love both one's parents (King or Queen) or, indeed, hate them (opponent's King and Queen)? The possibility of equally plausible symbolic permutations seems quite large here. Furthermore, in *The Psychology of Gambling* (1974), Jon Halliday and Peter Fuller include Ernest Jones' account of Morphy as an example of Freudian accounts of unresolved Oedipal urges in all games and gambling. It may be true that successful chess players often have within them an Oedipal complex (like most men), but even if we accept that view of things, there is really nothing to suggest that chess is any different from any other competitive activity. No comparative studies have been conducted between chess masters, Go masters, draughts players and tiddlywinks experts.

Ernest Jones' study was at least devoted to the understanding of the psychological illness of one famous player, and for all the deficiencies it may possess it was done with the most scrupulous care and attention to detail. In the next work which concerns us the psychoanalytic net is flung over a much wider circle.

Reuben Fine, grandmaster, former contender for the world title (he declined the place offered to him in the 1948 tournament to decide the issue), author of the very influential *Basic Chess Endings* (1941) as well as many delightfully written books on chess, has now abandoned chess for the practice of psychoanalysis. (A critic once remarked that this was a great loss for chess and at best a draw for psychoanalysis.) *The Psychology of the Chess Player* (1967) contains interesting first-hand observations about famous players, and considerable speculation about their personalities which, in the words of the Soviet psychologist and grandmaster Krogius (1976), is 'hard to believe'. But one of Fine's observations is rather interesting. As we saw in Chapter 2, chess is often hailed as an art, and yet, unlike the world of Art, there appears to be very much less overt homosexuality in the chess world compared to the art world. This, in itself, would be of little interest, but it would be consistent with the assumed prevalence of repressed homosexuality which some psychoanalysts have claimed is the motivating force in serious chess.

According to Fine, the whole game is seen as suffused with phallic symbolism. In particular the King is supremely important. It represents (a) the boy's penis in a phallic stage, (b) the essential characteristics of the self-image, and (c) the father pulled down to the boy's size. Similarly, the checkmate – the King under attack and with no legal move – reflects (a) castration, (b) the exposure of the concealed weakness, and (c) the destruction of the father.

These are, as it were, the axioms of the theory, and they generate, in what seems a rather undisciplined way, a wealth of lavish interpretations about anything connected with chess and its practitioners. They range from the amusing to the banal, and some seem slightly dotty. Let us illustrate our evaluations.

There are two opening variations associated with Lasker's name: the Exchange Variation in the Ruy Lopez, and Lasker's Defence in the Queen's Gambit Declined. What have they got in common? An unusually early exchange of Queens. 'To clarify the situation', says Fine, 'Lasker gets rid of women from his life'. This seems quite amusing because a much more rational explanation of Lasker's choice of these variations would be that both are consistent with the quiet way he often treated the openings. Equally droll is the account of Howard Staunton, who kept evading a match with Morphy. Once it is discovered he was a distinguished Shakespearean scholar, it follows that: 'Only the King of writers could attract his pen'. In the same vein, the title of one of his books, *Unsuspected Corruptions of Shakespeare's Text*, is regarded as a significant move in the protection of his King. And so it goes on. Capablanca had an oral fixation, and Alekhine, in whose presence the name of Capablanca must never be mentioned, was the sadist of the chess world. Of course, we knew a lot of this already. Alekhine's extraordinary war-time articles, setting out to prove that 'Jewish chess' is defensive and decadent, were somewhat sadistic, as was much of his behaviour. From the methodological point of view, however, we can see how easily the tenets of psychoanalytic theory can be flexibly twisted to fit each particular concrete case. This is like the responses of a mental medium in a seance who can so adeptly seize, or drop, a remark made by the sitters. The axioms of the theory do nothing to restrict the scope of the interpretations. At other times Fine's observations are wholly unspectacular. The 'tension' or 'nervousness' evinced by players before a crucial game is shared by most of us before an interview, or test of our wits, and is hardly related in any unique way to the onset of parricidal fantasies. But one example of such fantasy is curiously overlooked by Fine. The sixteenth-century Spanish priest Ruy Lopez advised the chess player to place the board in such a way that the sun would shine into his opponent's eyes. There is a classic

Freudian connection here which should have been irresistible. Ever since the Oedipus Myth was taken over by Freud, blindness was considered symbolic (by upwards displacement) of castration.

There are a few other contributions to the psychoanalytic literature concerned with chess, but they do not add a great deal to Fine's account. One strange book, *Idle Passion: Chess and the Dance of Death* by Alexander Cockburn (1975), incidentally neither a master nor an analyst, should be mentioned because it sets out to persuade us that chess is basically decadent. It is well informed about chess history, and worth reading for some of the anecdotes, e.g. those about Marcel Duchamp, who gave up art for chess, and wrote a treatise on a difficult branch of endgame theory. Cockburn, who is leftish in politics, is particularly aggrieved that such a splendid revolutionary culture as existed originally in the Soviet Union should have taken up chess as a propaganda weapon and a vehicle of culture and educational achievement. This dislike of chess as being a waste of time and energy is rather puzzling until a little detective work is done, based on a chance remark in the preface: 'My father defeated me in our early games'. All is illuminated. The author has been deprived of those enriching parricidal fantasies (at a stroke, one might say) which provide the spur for playing chess. The self-conscious rejection of chess is a mere counter-phobic reaction to the very idea of father-murder. One does not have to be an analyst to see something significant in spirited attacks against an exercise which (at the same time) is hailed as trivial. Cockburn is the rare case of a person who simultaneously dislikes chess and is clearly obsessed by it. But analysts, such as Ernest Jones and Reuben Fine, have now alerted the chess player to the true nature of the dire motivations which lie behind his play; hence a marked ambivalence towards chess should be surprising only to the uninitiated. Would not such an attitude be predicted by theory?

It is worth saying a few words about the basic difficulty of applied psychoanalysis, as distinct from the use of the theory in individual therapy. Freud started it off with some fascinating and provocative studies of religious thought and artistic productions. And in his wake distinguished analysts, such as Ernest Jones, have turned their attention to works of literature. Perhaps the most plausible example is the interpretation of Hamlet's procrastination in Oedipal terms (Jones, 1954). But the danger in interpreting the words of the dead is that the observer is all too likely to become hypnotised by a particular theme, and hence struck by the force of merely confirming evidence which (in the nature of things) allows for no compensating disconfirmation. Experimental psychologists have demonstrated that individuals (including scientists) have a very strong tendency to acquire cumulative positive evidence for any belief, or explanation, which fits the data (Wason and Johnson-Laird, 1972). This process is unwitting and carries with it the compelling ring of truth – especially when the idea is false. Even so-called normal people, in an experimental situation, often reject evidence which suggests that their hypothesis is wrong. To return to chess; if one knows the salient features of a master's career, if one knows about his character traits, or even if one knows about the kind of chess he played, then that knowledge may suggest to the psychoanalyst a plausible interpretation, and that interpretation will further unconsciously select more striking observations which confirm it. It may be the incompatible observations which are simply not seen. It is of some interest to note here that Fine's *own* free associations about the world of chess, in his book *The World's Best Chess Games* (1953), paint a nostalgic picture of its prominent personalities without much hint of the darker motives which are assumed to inform their passionate activities. Perhaps these motives have been censored by the author in the interests of what the readers want to know.

In this chapter we have ranged widely over disparate attempts to pin down factors connected with talent and motivation in chess. It is clear that no coherent picture has emerged, and it is unfortunate that research on motivation (as distinct from talent) has been almost entirely dominated by psychoanalytic speculation. The empirical research on talent, fragmentary though it is, suggests that (contrary to popular belief) there is little evidence that a chess player must be 'brainy'. Indeed, a good case could be made out for chess ability being a highly specific skill unconnected with anything else (see Chapter 5). On the other hand, the nagging thought remains that chess skill may be correlated with some kind of spatial intelligence. It may be no accident that British masters (notably Alexander, Golombek and Milner-Barry) played a leading part in the cracking of the Enigma Code at Bletchley Park during the 1939-45 War. Such an exercise seems a unique concrete case of combinational ability motivated by a literal 'will to win' against a deadly enemy. But unfortunately it hardly follows that excellence in chess is prognostic of cryptographic skills. The relevance of a possible spatial factor deserves serious investigation. It is reported that Bobby Fischer has revealed phenomenal expertise on the '15 puzzle', and the formidable Rubik Cube could be a test between chess players and the rest of the world.

In the absence of further empirical data we suggest that people play chess, not just to 'see the other fellow's ego crack', nor even to engage in fantasies of father-murder, but because they get an enduring satisfaction from formulating and solving difficult problems. It is here that experimental psychologists have made the most impressive advance in the understanding of chess skill. We consider it in Chapter 5.

4 Winning and Losing

The career path of a successful chess player is hard to predict for it may take several different courses, some smooth, others more bumpy. Normally we would expect any player destined to become a challenger for the world championship to have made his mark internationally while still in his teens and to have secured grandmaster status in his early twenties at the latest. There would follow a gradual improvement until a peak is reached between the ages of thirty and forty, followed by a slow but inexorable decline, becoming more steep after the age of fifty. That is the average pattern, but just as chess history is littered with youthful prodigies who may or may not fulfil their early promise, one may also cite those veteran prodigies who continue to produce top-class results in their fifties and beyond. Why then do some players reach their peak earlier than others, and why do some suffer a quick and drastic decline while others are able to stay at the top for decades? The answer is a complex relationship between ageing and motivation.

As a chess player grows older his physical stamina decreases, and with it his ability to sustain concentration over long periods. This is generally assumed to be the primary, or indeed the only reason for deterioration in his results. But experience is also an important factor in chess success. The more experienced player can rely on technique to a greater extent; he can play from knowledge, so should be able to expend less energy in calculation. There is no *a priori* reason to predict, solely on the basis of a decline in stamina, as consistent a pattern as undoubtedly exists in the deterioration of playing strength of older players. We would argue that a decline in motivation is at least as important a factor affecting performance, particularly when a player has achieved those goals which he set himself in his youth.

Motivation is a notoriously difficult factor to measure with any degree of precision or reliability, but a study of the results of world championship standard chess players over long periods of their careers does throw considerable light on the relationships between age, motivation and results. A paper by Norman R.Draper (1963), entitled 'Does Age Affect Master Chess?', included two interesting statistical analyses connected with this theme. His first conclusion is based on an examination of the relative ages of contestants in all the world championship matches from Morphy-Anderssen 1858 until Botvinnik-Tal 1961 (the early matches before 1886 were included as being generally accepted as world title contests if not officially recognised as such). His hypothesis was simply that the older man in such matches stands no worse chance than his opponent. A simple statistical test showed no reason to doubt the hypothesis. There is, however, much reason to doubt whether we should take much notice of this result. The habit of the pre-war champions to defend their title against chosen opponents makes the statistics somewhat suspect, as does Botvinnik's practice of losing and regaining the title in successive years. We shall have more to say about world championship matches and the motivation surrounding them.

Far more interesting than his analysis of match results was Draper's study of the tournament records of seven great players. The life-time results of Tarrasch, Lasker, Nimzowitsch, Tartakower, Réti, Capablanca and Alekhine were examined in five-year age bands. Examination of the figures brought out two interesting features: firstly that overall scores did not drop alarmingly as players aged (Tarrasch and Capablanca were the worst in this respect but the others showed no marked deterioration), and secondly that, on the whole, the grandmasters tended to win proportionately fewer, lose proportionately about the same number and draw proportionately more games as their age increased. The tables do not indicate overall that advancing age brings on a sudden flurry of losses. Draper continues: 'They do appear to suggest that the older player is, perhaps, not so able to press home a winning advantage and is, or must be, content with more draws'. Perhaps the crucial question here is whether he truly *is* content with that state of affairs or merely *must be*. There is also no evidence to suggest that a higher proportion of the draws later in a player's career are indeed a result of his failing to press home an advantage. They could equally well be a result of his failing to achieve such a desirable state in the first place.

Draper advances an explanation of the career data based on the following two points: firstly, that as a player grows older his style becomes better known and opponents find it easier to prepare for him; and secondly, that he willingly rejects risky moves in the knowledge that increasing age brings susceptibility to fatigue and the possibility of calculational error.

Neither of these points is fully convincing. Young players frequently have far more limited repertoires than their seniors and consequently should be easier to prepare for (though perhaps preparation was a harder task in olden times when there were considerably fewer tournaments than there are nowadays). Moreover, is there any evidence that older players reject risk-taking because they are conscious of the possibility of error? Is there indeed any reason to believe that older players miscalculate more frequently in tactically complex positions than in simple ones? According to the theory of ageing bringing tiredness, we might even recommend risky play to older players in order to ensure that the critical point of a game is reached early in the playing session when they are still strong enough to deal with it. Older players do appear to be less willing to take risks, but the reasons for their reluctance are deeper then those outlined above. To understand the position better we need to comprehend a chess player's Fear of Losing.

There are two priorities for any contestant in a chess game: to win, if possible, and to avoid defeat. (For some amateurs, of course, it matters not who won or lost . . . but here we are dealing with the serious competitors.) For most players, the misery of defeat is greater than the elation of victory. But for the pleasure of the spectators, we might even deduce that chess increases the net amount of unhappiness in the world. For some players, the pain of defeat is so high that throughout their careers they appear to strive not so much for success, but for the avoidance of failure. Rarely willing to take risks, they prefer a safe draw to a venture into the unknown with the chance of victory. The avoidance of risk is not based on any supposed chance of miscalculation, but on a distaste for entering the incalculable. Such a tendency may be seen in some players of all ages. Generally, however, the young player is ambitious and willing to suffer a little on the road to glory. The occasional defeat can be tolerated, as long as there are enough victories in compensation. As a player adds to his list of battle honours, his appetite for victory wanes. Ambitions are achieved and further glories just add more trophies to a well-stocked sideboard. But the pain of defeat and the misery of failure never retreat. Particularly when a player has scaled great peaks in the chess world, a defeat by a lesser man has an element of humiliation. The fear of losing grows as an eminent player grows older. The temptation to settle for a comfortable life of painless draws may become harder to resist. We would cite many cases of grandmasters who in their prime were candidates for the world championship but rapidly thereafter underwent a metamorphosis into 'drawing masters'. The cause is not the peacefulness of old age, but the the comparative loss of attraction of glory compared with the suffering of failure.

The effect of success on motivation is difficult to predict. Players will consciously or subconsciously set themselves goals to achieve in their chess career. As soon as a goal is achieved, it is generally superseded by a higher goal. For some time an ambitious young player might think it all-important that he win his local club championship. Once that has been achieved, he sets his sights on the county championship, then the national championship. What is important is that another target should immediately present itself and should appear to be attainable within a reasonable period of time. We shall refer again to this problem of finding attainable goals in Chapter 10, in discussing the possible reasons for the failure of women players to reach the highest echelons of chess. Here we consider the tragic case of the player who can set himself no more goals – the world champion.

Hardly a single world champion in the history of chess has continued to play as well after winning the title as he did on his path to the throne. When Anatoly Karpov won the grandmaster tournament at Ljubljana and Portorož in 1975, one journalist claimed it to be the first time in forty-one years that a world champion had secured an undivided first place in a major international event. (The claim may easily be disputed on the grounds of what does or does not constitute a major event, but that such a claim can be made at all is remarkable enough.) Of course there is a temptation to relax after winning the world championship. Life is easier and appearance fees are high, but where is the motivation for further victories to be found? A world champion must work as hard as before just to retain his position; no further goals beckon.

The post-war history of the world championship is a saga of under-achievement by the champions, beginning with Mikhail Botvinnik, who won the title convincingly in 1948 but could only reproduce his best form in return matches after losing to his challengers. Smyslov, Tal, Petrosian and Spassky all appeared to suffer a loss of form as soon as they won the championship, while Bobby Fischer avoided the problem by a self-imposed exile from active play, beginning the moment he became world champion.

Perhaps that was the accident which explains Karpov's unique achievement. After winning Fischer's title by default, he still had something left to prove. The only champion who had gained the title in such a manner, he still retained his motivation. Yet his continued willingness to compete in the strongest events and his continued appetite for further victories shows motivation of an exceptionally high order.

Let us return to the question of the age at which a chess player might be expected to reach his peak. Leaving aside the important factor of motivation, we find ourselves considering the conflict between increasing experience and decreasing stamina as a player ages. As the number of international tournaments has increased throughout chess history, and the literature available has also proliferated, experience has been more easily obtained by the improving player. We would therefore expect the peak age to have lowered, and this is indeed the case. Fifty years ago most of the world's leading grandmasters were around forty years of age. Already many of the top players are in their twenties or younger. In 1936 Fred Reinfeld, writing in *Chess* magazine, declared: 'I think I am safe . . . in stating that the best part of the average chess master's life is between the ages of 36 and 42. He has then had time to temper the virility of youth with experience, while old age has not begun to affect his powers to any perceptible extent'. Yet Reinfeld predicted that the age of maturity of a chess player would decrease. Whereas the master of previous generations had taken ten or fifteen years to develop judgment and technique, the younger masters of the 1930s quickly absorbed the lessons of Tarrasch and Capablanca. The apprenticeship to grandmasterhood has already dropped to five or six years and today is perhaps still less.

The competition for the world championship provides a convenient opportunity to study the ages at which great players have reached their peak. Since 1948 the championship has been decided by a series of eliminating competitions to determine an eventual

challenger every three years to meet the titleholder. By noting how
far a player has reached along the qualifying road, we can obtain a
good idea of his place in the world championship hierarchy. To
establish himself as a genuine contender for the title, any player's
ambition is to reach the 'Candidates' stage, the last eight of the
qualifiers who must undergo a final eliminating series before the
world championship match. The following table lists recent
Candidates who have undoubtedly figured among the top ten players
in the world, but have subsequently performed less successfully. The
table lists the year of their highest world championship placing and
their age at that time. The final column is the age at which they first
appeared in the 'top ten'.

Name	Best Year	Age	Early Peak
Smyslov	1957	36	29
Keres	1953	37	22
Boleslavsky	1950	31	22
Bronstein	1951	27	25
Najdorf	1950	40	40(?)
Kotov	1950	37	37
Stahlberg	1950	42	42(?)
Reshevsky	1948	37	25
Petrosian	1966	37	24
Geller	1962	37	28
Gligorić	1959	36	36
Spassky	1969	32	19
Tal	1960	24	23
Fischer	1972	29	16
Olafsson	1959	24	24
Benko	1962	34	31
Korchnoi	1978	47	31
Larsen	1965	30	30

Some of these dates for 'best year' might be open to argument. For example, Paul Keres managed to maintain his high point for a decade, securing second place in four consecutive Candidates tournaments; Gligorić, after apparently reaching a peak in 1959, attained a comparable level in 1968. Finally, the performance of Portisch is not included in the table, because, at the time of writing, his decline has not yet begun. He reached the Candidates first in 1965 at the age of 28, but his best results to date have been in 1977 and 1980.

The table draws attention to two factors of ageing. First, the surprising diversity of age at which a player's peak is reached. (We notice, however, that it is becoming increasingly uncommon for a player to improve after the age of thirty.) Second, the long time interval which may elapse between first appearance in the Candidates and eventual deterioration in results. Spassky, Fischer and Petrosian all needed thirteen years at the highest level before making the final breakthrough to become world champions, though at the other extreme we should observe that both Tal and Karpov won the title at their first attempt.

With such different career paths, any generalisations may easily be contradicted. A grandmaster may reach his peak at any age between 24 and 47 and can maintain a level of play at or near his best for up to fifteen years, or perhaps longer. And when the deterioration begins, it is generally a slow process. Like old soldiers, chess players just fade away. One of the more remarkable feats of recent world championship history is Viktor Korchnoi's refusal to fade away after the age of 45. Clearly the normal process of ageing has failed to take its toll. The natural explanation for his unnatural behaviour must be linked to his decision to defect from the USSR. His change of country, subsequent political battles and intense animosity towards former compatriots have been widely acclaimed as responsible for his sudden late surge. Certainly there was no doubting his intense motivation during the Candidates matches of 1977 and 1980. To some extent a valid comparison may be made with other players who have left the Soviet Union. Their results make an interesting study. We must remember that in the USSR the state supports professional chess players; when they make their life in the West, winning may become a matter of financial necessity. The following table shows the career progress of seven grandmasters who changed country in this manner. The ratings are based on a statistical analysis of results, taking into account the strength of opposition. As a rough guide, the average rating for international master is 2400, for grandmaster 2500, for world championship candidate 2600, and the world champion is usually around 2700. The figures given here represent the ratings of the named players in the years surrounding their emigration, beginning three years before.

Name + Age on leaving USSR	Rating in year:								
	D–3	D–2	D–1	D	D+1	D+2	D+3	D+4	D+5
Alburt 32	2520	2505	2510	2515	2515	2575	2550		
Ivanov 33	2415	2415	2430	2430	2515				
Korchnoi 45	2650	2670	2665	2670	2645	2665	2695	2695	2650
Lein 46	2540	2535	2515	2525	2505	2535	2520	2485	2485
Liberzon 38	2540	2515	2515	2485	2540	2550	2555	2515	2545
Shamkovich 51	2535	2540	2505	2505	2485	2485	2485	2495	2515
Jinjihashvili 32	2520	2525	2525	2535	2550	2595	2570	2490	2450

The pattern suggested by these figures is that of marked improvement within the space of two or three years after emigration, followed by an equally rapid decline sometimes even to a level below the original base. Only Shamkovich and to a lesser extent Lein do not follow this pattern; perhaps they may be excused on grounds of age. We have yet to see whether Ivanov, with youth on his side, will be able to maintain his advance. At the very least, the table shows that change of country and culture can have a profound effect on motivation and results.

Other sudden changes in life pattern can also have their effect on the careers of chess players. Some experience a marked deterioration in results after marriage, though that same change of state can result in equally marked improvement in others. Such observations add to the evidence that changes in a player's level of performance over time are more influenced by factors affecting motivation than simple ageing.

The final stages of careers of great players make an interesting study on their own. For many, their love of the game causes them to continue playing competitively with gradually deteriorating results. The same is true of those professional players who know no other trade. Other grandmasters react more drastically by retiring from competition when they finally admit that their results no longer merit the expenditure of further energy. Those who seem never to have lost their lust for battle have produced some remarkable feats of chess longevity. The two most astonishing achievements in this direction must be Emanuel Lasker's third place at Moscow 1935 at the age of 66, and Vassily Smyslov's qualification for the Candidates tournament in 1982 at the age of 61. For Smyslov this marked a return to the forefront of world championship competition which he first graced 35 years previously. One cannot imagine any other sport in which a man can remain in the top ten in the world for such a length of time.

At the present time chess is more a young man's game than ever before, yet the older masters still survive at the top. Nevertheless, the change which international chess has undergone in recent years has without doubt made life at the top more intense and consequently more demanding of energy and youthful vigour. Two factors above all have changed the character of the highest level of international competition. Firstly, the proliferation of chess literature has made the spread of theory and ideas much faster than in former times. Secondly, the number of really top-class tournaments has increased dramatically, leading to more encounters among the leading players and a consequent need for each of them to keep working to stay ahead in theoretical preparation. Gone are the days when a single well-analysed innovation could bring victory on several different occasions. Now the pace of chess communications is so fast that any important new game is already published throughout the world within weeks if not days. This theme is well illustrated by a rather curt exchange of views between two recent world champions. In 1979, Mikhail Botvinnik expressed the opinion that chessmasters of today play too much and care too little about theory, preparation and the game itself. Anatoly Karpov (1980) answered this charge as follows:

> It is sad that such a great master as Botvinnik does not understand modern chess. He withdrew from active chess years ago when you did not need to play nearly as much as now. He exploited the slow spreading of chess news around the world. Having spotted a good idea he was able to use it even perhaps for a whole year until other players were able to defend themselves against it. When I come up with something new, the whole world will know the following week. You have to continue playing in order not to fall behind. I find this development very positive as it forces you towards activity and new research all the time.

Remembering that Botvinnik only retired from international tournament play in 1970, this gives a good picture of how much the chess world has changed in a decade. Writing of his last few years in active competition, Botvinnik (1981) admitted: '. . . from a creative point of view I had to live mainly on my "old research fat". And I played fairly successfully, because I employed systems which had been studied and prepared before 1963'.

If we are to accept Karpov's doctrine, continuous play at the highest levels is necessary to remain at the top. More than ever before stamina is demanded in great measure for chess success. The older grandmaster may have the strength for single games, or even to play whole tournaments with the vigour of his youth, but the continuous grind of international contests must take its toll. We should not have been surprised at Smyslov's success in the 1982 Interzonal tournament. A great player and former world champion can prepare for a single tournament, ensuring enough fresh ammunition to give him good chances of victory. But to maintain the heavy work-load necessary to keep on top of the theoretical battle ought to be too much to ask for a sexagenarian.

We have frequently referred to the strong effect motivation can have on a player's results, but it is not enough to be strongly motivated to win. A chess player must also have confidence in his ability to do so. Self-esteem is an important and delicate component of the grandmaster, liable to sustain damage after any defeat. Over-confidence brings its own dangers of recklessness and lack of care, but a loss of belief in his own abilities is the greater enemy.

A sensible reaction to defeat is something which every player has to develop. Some will make a special effort to win the following game, others will consolidate slowly, taking precautions above all to avoid further painful losses. In his *Chessplayer's Psychological Preparation* (Moscow, 1979), Krogius gives an interesting table comparing the results of various world class players in games following a loss. Taking all their important tournaments and matches after attaining grandmaster status, he calculates percentage scores in games immediately after defeats. Karpov and Lasker emerge as the most resilient players, on 67.8 per cent and 65.1 per cent respectively. At the other end of the scale Fischer (50 per cent) and Euwe (42.5 per cent) appear to have suffered most by defeat. Unfortunately Krogius does not provide us with the overall scores of the players concerned in the events under consideration, so we have no precise measure of how well or badly they reacted to defeat in comparison with their normal performance. The surprisingly low scores of Fischer and Euwe, however, do demonstrate the unsettling effect a loss can have.

Particularly shattering can be a bad loss in match play. Several world championship aspirants have never recovered from a single match defeat. In particular, Bobby Fischer's convincing series of victories which took him to the world championship in 1972 seemed to sap the will of a whole generation of players. In the decade that followed, none of those players defeated by Fischer was able to recover his previous form.

Perhaps the worst fate for an aspiring chess player is that he should become accustomed to losing. It is a habit of which it can be hard to rid oneself. A series of losses to a particular opponent can establish a 'pecking order' which is repeated on later occasions. Grandmasters can be heard referring to their favourite 'clients' or 'customers' – other grandmasters who can be relied upon to donate a full point in their encounters. A moral ascendency is established by previous encounters and the underdog feels lost from the start.

Occasionally one even meets such a trio of players that Grandmaster A is confident of victory against Grandmaster B, who in turn feels sure to win against Grandmaster C. Yet all three are of approximately equal strength, and Grandmaster C always wins against A. There was an amusing example of such a circumstance during the BBC Master Game tournament in 1978. Miles, Hort and Larsen must all have felt that the result of this knock-out event would be determined by the initial draw since Miles had an excellent record against Larsen, who in turn had some good recent results against Hort, who could boast several wins against Miles. Hort duly eliminated Miles in the semi-final and went on to lose to Larsen in the final. Miles proved his point by beating Larsen in the first round of the following year's competition.

As a final example of the extent to which losing can damage your chess health, we should like to mention the tragic finish to a game between Larsen and Gheorghiu at the chess Olympics in Siegen in 1970. In the years before that game, Larsen had amassed such a collection of wins against the Romanian grandmaster that Gheorghiu found it hard to play against him at all. Finally, however, in the position shown he seemed sure to end his sequence of defeats. With the black pieces, Gheorghiu to move has an extra knight and is

set to win comfortably with 39 ... ♘f3, with the threat of 40 ... ♘g5 mate. Let Keene and Levy take up the story from their book on the tournament (1970):

Eyewitnesses present at the closing stages of this amazing encounter allege that Gheorghiu reached out his hand to administer the lethal blow 39 ... N-B6, but at this precise moment the said hand was seized with a convulsive tremble which rendered the Romanian grandmaster incapable of transferring the piece to the required square. In the act of summoning up sufficient reserves of will-power to overcome this unfortunate and paralytic state of affairs, Black overstepped the time limit.

It could not have happened with any other opponent.

5 The Essential Patterns

'How many moves can you see ahead?'. All chess players have been asked this question at one time or another by the eager layman. The answer is assumed to be a rough index of competence. 'As a rule, not a single one', replied Réti, thereby perhaps hoping to demolish at a blow the stereotyped assumption. In *Modern Ideas in Chess* (1923) he continues with an apt analogy: ' . . . The power of accurately calculating moves in advance has no greater place in chess than, perhaps, skilful calculation has in mathematics'. He knew what he was talking about – he had abandoned a career in mathematics for one in chess.

But if it is not a matter of seeing ahead, of exact calculation, then what, it may be asked, constitutes the phenomenal powers of the master? The answer – and it is a surprising one – was first unequivocally demonstrated in a voluminous book by Adrian de Groot (1965), who is both a master (he played in the Dutch team in the 1937 Olympiad) and a professional psychologist. The odd thing about this book is that its justly famous influence on subsequent research is accounted for by one experiment which is described in thirteen of its 440 pages – a mere three per cent of the whole. As a chess master on friendly terms with many of the world's leading grandmasters, and as an experimental psychologist with a laboratory at his command, de Groot was ideally equipped to carry out the most celebrated investigation of chess skill ever conducted.

The vast bulk of the research reported in the book, however, consisted in 'protocol analyses', based on the technique of 'thinking aloud', when the subject is required to choose (and justify) the continuation in a middle game position taken from master games. The analyses extracted in this manner make fascinating reading for the chess player, especially when it is remembered that the grandmaster subjects included Keres, Alekhine, Flohr, Fine and Euwe. But, on the whole, the results were scientifically disappointing. There appeared to be nothing in the gross thought processes which distinguishes playing strength. Grandmasters and masters search about as deeply as lesser players – if anything, they consider fewer alternatives before deciding on the best continuation. In fact, the one reliable difference seems tautological: masters invariably explore strong moves while weaker players spend considerable time analysing the consequences of bad moves. How could it be otherwise unless one clings to the naive assumption that the master's skill resides *solely* in more powerful calculation? A running record of a master's thought processes may be of interest to the chess player but baffling to the psychologist, especially when the attempt is made to interpret it in terms of Selz's theory of thinking, which even psychologists find difficult to understand. Perhaps the master is seeing more, as we have hinted in previous chapters. Thoughts of this kind may have been in de Groot's mind when he hit upon the simple idea of the board reconstruction experiment which has become the prototype of all subsequent research on chess thinking. Like all profound ideas one wonders why nobody had thought of it before. The essence of chess skill is captured, not in a deliberate consideration of how the game might continue, but in how a position is structured in the first few seconds of seeing it.

The seminal experiment, carried out in 1944, consisted in exposing a middle game position on a board for between two and ten seconds, and then asking individuals to reconstruct it on an empty board. Only four subjects were used: a grandmaster (Euwe), a master, an expert, and a 'representative for the weaker class of players'. However, a series of different trials was employed, the material consisting of sixteen diverse positions, randomly picked from relatively obscure master games. When the exposure of a position was terminated, the subjects were (rather oddly) encouraged to organize the material mentally, i.e. consolidate it, for about half a minute. The grandmaster and master then dictated the position, while the weaker players set about reconstructing the board, and at the same time giving an introspective commentary. In all cases a rather complicated scoring system was used to assess performance.

The results were dramatic. The accuracy of reconstruction varied as a positive function of skill. Not much difference was found between grandmaster and master, but there was a striking difference between master and expert, 91.4 per cent correct as opposed to 69.6 per cent correct, and the poor 'weaker player' achieved only 52.5 per cent. Qualitatively, the most interesting result, which was apparent from the introspective protocols, was that at the grandmaster and master levels the positions were perceived in large complexes, e.g. a castled position, a particular type of pawn structure, a group of co-ordinating pieces etc.

As we shall see, this type of experiment has been replicated to such a large extent that it has virtually become a paradigm for psychological research into chess skill. These replications confirm the supposition that the superiority of the master is not due simply to the memory of the specific position which was presented in the test, but to a vast store of previous experience with *analogous* positions. This process, however, is extremely complicated. De Groot states: 'The Master does not *calculate* more than the Expert . . . : the Master *sees* more than the Expert, especially the more important things'. The concept of 'seeing' seems very different from that of 'calculating', and yet it seems likely that the former may involve an extremely rapid inferential process, including the rejection of bad moves, which is not adequately covered by the term 'calculation'. And it certainly seems true that, as in other kinds of skilled performance, introspection (or retrospection) only encompasses a fraction of the thought processes involved. It was almost certainly for this reason that the old 'find the continuation' type of experiment, initially used by de Groot to study the master's thought processes, almost faded from view, so far as the psychologist is concerned. The credit for refining the technique and for its theoretical elaboration goes to William Chase and Herbert Simon of Carnegie-Mellon University. These investigators not only devised important experimental controls which enabled de Groot's original ideas to be tested more accurately, they substituted a more rigorous theoretical language for discussing them than Selz's rather vague formulations.

'It seems rather obvious to me', said a master of our acquaintance. He thereby did little more than display an unwitting knowledge of how he would have performed in the task. A high degree of skill of any kind is usually tacit rather than explicit, e.g. the non-writer is often struck in wonderment by what is taken to be the effortless abilities of the seasoned writer. The sceptic, however, might question not so much the ease with which the board is reconstructed, but the nature of the powers behind such a feat. It might be argued that all that has been demonstrated is a superior ability to remember which pieces belong on which squares, and that this may be attributed to superior general powers of memory. After all, hasn't it always been the chess master's astonishing memory which has attracted investigators from Binet onwards? In 1925 Djakow, Rudik and Petrowski had been specifically interested in the master's alleged powers of memory, but unfortunately they used an absurdly long exposure time (one minute), and they presented a chess problem (rather than a game position), which would have been totally remote from any chess playing experience. To make matters worse, their control group consisted of non-players, and hence any comparison would have been *a priori* biased. It is like comparing the literary appreciation of established novelists with that of students who attend courses in creative writing. In spite of these criticisms of earlier research, it could still be argued (in principle) that de Groot's improvements in experimentation have done little to support the claim of a specific perceptual skill exercised by the master as a function of wealth of experience.

Chase and Simon (1973) resolved the sceptic's qualms: it is not a matter of any general superior memory. As usual, they got a master, an expert and a beginner to reconstruct positions from games, just as de Groot had done, but they also presented random positions (made up with the same pieces as the game positions) to be similarly reconstructed. The findings were decisive. With the random positions the differences in skill were abolished. All three subjects did equally badly – they did even worse than the beginner with the game positions. And yet the number of items to be retained in mind was constant – only their configuration differed. The inference is clear, and, like that in so many good experiments, it now seems obvious: the achievement of the master in the board reconstruction type of experiment is due to the experience of *similar* constellations of pieces already structured in long-term memory. The board is not reconstructed *ab initio* – the exposed position is unconsciously seen as a corrected version of a prototype. It follows that the new information – the given position on the board – is essentially an adjustment to a known pattern. (Psychologists at this point will recall a famous phrase coined by Woodworth as early as 1938: 'schema plus correction'.) We shall consider a formulation of this process in more detail in a moment, but its rapid nature is made evident by one interesting, unpublished, observation. A German psychologist, Friedric Friedel, told us (personal communication) that he exposed to strong players a mixture of positions (a) from unknown games, and (b) from well-known master games. The task was simply to make known as quickly as possible whether they recognized each position. The result showed that an exposure interval of 0.8 seconds was sufficient to make this discrimination accurately. According to Friedel, his fellow psychologists claimed that such speed was impossible in view of the amount of information to be processed.

It is worth recording here a few technical innovations introduced by the American workers, but first we should note that the idea of using random positions as a control was first implemented by Lemmens and Jongman in the Amsterdam Laboratory (unpublished). It will be remembered, too, that in the original de Groot experiment the reconstruction of a given position was attempted in a single trial. Chase and Simon measured performance over a series of repeated trials, i.e. if the first attempt was not correct, the subject was told what was wrong and allowed to inspect the position again before attempting a second reconstruction. In addition, they devised a new kind of task (the 'perception task') to supplement the results from the original 'memory task'. In this new task a game position was set up on one board and the task was simply to reproduce it on an empty adjacent board with a new set of chessmen, and of course to do it as quickly as possible. This allowed the experimenter to measure both the number of head movements made in glancing between the two boards and the number of men placed on the new board after each 'look back' at the given position. The technique allowed the definition of the basic units of chess perception – 'chunks', i.e. not individual pieces, but local clusters of pieces of the same colour which usually defend each other. It was assumed that when the player looks back at the original position he will have encoded only a single 'chunk' which is then reproduced on the other board. It was found that the master took only a second, or two, to gather new information, whereas the beginner took about four seconds. It was further shown, by integrating the information derived from both tasks, that the master not only recalled larger 'chunks', but also more of them. For further information the interested reader is referred to Chase and Simon (1973).

So far we have discussed only the demonstration of a phenomenon.

We turn now to some theoretical accounts which purport to explain it, and which are more powerful than the rather old-fashioned, and perhaps untestable, ideas developed by the original investigators. These accounts are somewhat technical, but we shall try to present them without running the risk of too much simplification.

Chase and Simon (1973) formulated an 'information processing theory' which draws heavily upon computer programs designed to simulate human performance. The skill of a master is assumed to be basically one of 'pattern recognition', and the theory is tested by seeing how well a program matches it. First, the theory assumes a very large repertoire of patterns stored in long-term memory, i.e. what is already known from experience. Such patterns constitute a master's vocabulary, and it is estimated that its size lies between 10,000 and 100,000, which is about as large as a good reader's recognition vocabulary. A 'word' in chess language corresponds to a 'chunk', i.e. familiar, over-learned constellations of pieces such as pawn chains, fianchettoes, 'weak colour complexes', open files, backward pawns, potential forks and pins etc etc. It has been demonstrated that a computer simulation with about 1,000 patterns in store recognized only fifty per cent of quiet positions in a five-second recall task (Simon and Gilmartin, 1973). Second, the theory assumes a mechanism to access these patterns called EPAM (Elementary Perceiver and Memorizer). This is a discrimination net, or set of instructions, so that the perceptual system can scan the board systematically. At the end of each path in this net is stored the 'internal name', or label, representing the pattern that was discovered, or perceived, by following that path. In addition, a short-term memory, of limited capacity, stores the names, or labels, of the patterns which have been retrieved. Finally, another system, PERCEIVER, based on the processes that determine eye movements over the board, is assumed to make a preliminary scan to detect salient pieces.

The postulation of these systems may sound unduly complicated and extravagant, but their necessity is founded on the belief of those who work in artificial intelligence that no mental process can be assumed, or taken for granted, unless it can be strictly formulated in terms of mechanisms which (in principle) could be realized in a computer program. In fact, Chase and Simon stress that the theory is really very simple (as these things go):

The salient piece detector (PERCEIVER) first derives a list of salient pieces, rank-ordered from highest down. Each salient piece is sorted in turn through the EPAM net and the label of the pattern that is recognized is stored in short-term memory. This label can be thought of as representing both (internally) a path through the EPAM net and (externally) a cluster of pieces about the salient piece. This recognition process continues until attention has been directed to all the salient pieces, or the short-term memory is filled with labels. Finally, in recall, the labels from short-term memory are used to derive from the EPAM net the information about the location of pieces in the 'chunk', and the result is the reproduction of each pattern that has been recognized.

The theory has been fairly well empirically tested. With a repertoire of about 1000 patterns in store the simulation was found to perform as well as an expert (US Class A player), but significantly worse than a master. The extrapolation of between 10,000 and 100,000 patterns, which might suffice to equal the skill of mastership, is quite plausible. Indeed, the notion of master chess as a highly developed form of 'pattern recognition' has now inspired a number of studies (mainly in the USA and Canada) in the information-processing tradition. The basic idea, that skilled chess is due to access to a vast number of stored patterns, appears to be incontrovertible; no other kind of explanation is likely to account for the rapidity of initial perception. A couple of other studies are worth mentioning in this connection. The Soviet physiologist V.Malkin (1982) reported an experiment in the magazine 64 which demonstrated how the critical idea in a position can dominate perception. Instead of exposing 'quiescent' positions, as de Groot had done, Malkin employed tactical positions which allowed a unique combinative solution. The subjects were instructed first to find this solution, and *then* to reproduce the board. As might now be expected, a couple of grandmasters (Tal and Vasyukov) solved with rapidity and reconstructed with accuracy, but a master and a candidate master both achieved the solution in slightly longer time, and were unable to reproduce with accuracy a piece which played no part in the combination; in fact, it was restored on a conventional, stereotyped square where it seemed it 'ought to belong'. Malkin argues quite cogently that this phenomenon is at the root of 'chess blindness' and 'blunders'. In psychological terms, a configuration to which attention is not paid may fall outside a stored pattern, and its correction seems irrelevant to the play (see Chapter 7). The other study, an unpublished project by Mary Goss (1982), is of some interest because it showed a significant difference between players and non-players in the reconstruction of random positions. Thus it differed from the classical results of Chase and Simon who used such positions as controls for any general memory, or past experience. But the error was to allow far too long an exposure time (one minute), thus copying the technique of Djakow, Rudik and Petrowski (1926). Of some interest, however, was the inclusion of intelligence tests (and specifically tests of spatial intelligence), and these showed no difference whatsoever between the two groups.

More critical for the established theory of chess as pattern recognition is an experiment by Holding and Reynolds (1982) who also employed random (but legal) positions. As subjects they tested not masters but graded US players. However, in addition to the reconstruction of the positions (which were exposed for eight seconds), the experimenters introduced a new procedure: they required the players to evaluate the positions and suggest the best continuations.

As expected, there were no differences between the different classes of player in the ability to reconstruct the random positions. So much is entirely consistent with the 'pattern recognition hypothesis'. However, clear differences were obtained in the efficiency with which the positions were evaluated – the better the player the better the analysis. And a difference of this kind cannot be attributed to accessing a long-term memory store of familiar patterns because positions generated in a random generator cannot be familiar.

This result may be seen as casting doubt on any strong form of the recognition-association theory in which pattern memory, as conventionally estimated by the brief recall task, is assumed to be solely responsible for differences in chess skill. However, as the authors admit, a weaker form of the theory, in which pattern memory is one component of chess skill, remains a distinct possibility. What the result does suggest is that, in addition to generating a set of initial moves, it is also necessary in playing chess to project a branching tree of replies and counter-moves until a 'quiescent' position is reached, and to evaluate the position thus obtained. As Holding and Reynolds make clear, this kind of analysis is more consistent with earlier attempts to program computers to play chess. Despite earlier findings, it does appear that differences exist in the depth of search between stronger and weaker players. But perhaps this is not really at all surprising, in that nobody would have supposed otherwise. It would be odd to appraise different components in chess skill in a different way. Of course, analysis occurs in chess, and, of course, we should expect the better player to be better at it. The perceptual ability, however, which determines the base for analysis, is a more fundamental ability. A great artist is distinguished by the way he sees things, and not by the way in which he applies the paint. One could even say it is the difference between vision and technique, both of which are critical for success or survival.

The idea of a dual process in chess thought has been formulated by the philosopher Hubert Dreyfus (1972) in his arguments which attempt to refute some of the claims made by research workers in artificial intelligence. He maintains that all the protocols obtained from experiments on chess thinking exhibit two distinct kinds of behaviour:

> (1) *zeroing in*, by means of the overall organization of the perceptual field, on an area formerly on the fringes of consciousness, and which other areas still on the fringes of consciousness make interesting; and (2) *counting out* explicit alternatives.

Dreyfus argues that (1) is not susceptible to the kind of digital information processing postulated by Chase and Simon. The battle of ideas between theorists in this field will go on for a long time, probably without a decisive victory for either side, but the existence of two stages – the first holistic (or intuitive) and the second analytical – has been corroborated in a variety of reasoning tasks (see Evans, 1982). Suppose we were to separate the skills involved in decision-making into calculation and judgment (although, of course, any calculation is liable to involve some judgmental skills). It seems reasonable to assume that the calculating part demands a certain degree of logical ability or intelligence. Beyond that necessary intelligence, the skill of calculation may be acquired by practice. On that assumption, we would expect to find that all good chess players are basically bright, but the greatest players not necessarily brighter than the merely strong, as indeed seems the case from personal observation.

Judgmental skills, on the other hand, seem to be largely based on pattern recognition functioning at two levels. First, one must have the ability to process, in an efficient manner, the experiences of previous games (and study) in order to form (probably unconsciously at least some of the time) those concepts which form the basis for judgments. Second, one must be able to recognize which of these preformed concepts are relevant in any given position. The formation of concepts may be a skill of 'pure pattern recognition', that of applying the concepts once formed is the clearly non-transferable part of chess ability.

At a low level, chess is largely calculation, and might therefore be a useful practice for logical skills. At a high level, it becomes more and more a matter of application of purely chess concepts, and so the practice is of no non-chess use whatsoever. Chess is a better mental exercise for weak players than for strong ones. The distinction between calculation and the ineffable 'positional instinct' is sometimes manifested even at the very highest level. Consider the contrast between a grandmaster who is usually thought of as predominantly a tactician and one who is usually thought of as predominantly a strategist. In his book on the 1960 World Championship, Tal (1977) quotes a dialogue after one game against Botvinnik. The latter, describing a crucial decision in the game, explained: 'At first I thought this position was better for White, but later I found the correct plan: I had to exchange rooks and keep queens on the board'. Tal goes on: 'At first such an evaluation of the position seemed to me rather abstract, but when I began to go over numerous variations I came to the conclusion that M.Botvinnik was absolutely correct'.

We might say that powerful application of profound principles enabled Botvinnik to reach a conclusion that Tal could only manage by a lengthy process of calculation. A conversation between players of different strengths sometimes goes like this, when the stronger player rejects a move suggested by a weaker one in a post mortem:

Weaker Player: What's wrong with it?
Stronger Player: It's not good.
Weaker Player: Why not?
Stronger Player: It's not the sort of move you play in this sort of position. *(End of Conversation)*

The situation is not untypical, and it is obvious that the two players begin their evaluations from two very different tacit premises. It all goes to show how communication between chess players of differing skill can break down because of a tacit, non-verbal component. But if such a skill permits of differing gradations, and varies with respect to a seemingly non-verbalizable component, then one keeps coming back to the perplexing question about whether it could be (or actually is) associated with a vehicle other than chess. It has been a more or less persistent finding throughout all the psychological investigations that chess players differ from non-players in neither general logical ability (as measured by tests), nor in powers of memory. Still, one view is that a very good chess player does have some mental quality that could be (perhaps more profitably?) devoted to other causes, and that the appropriate mental test to

> Every game of chess in a way is a contest of the nerves. Tournament play is essentially different from work in the quiet of one's own study, where you work when you feel so disposed and where you rest when you are tired; it is a relentless intellectual struggle before a numerous public, at a prescribed hour and with a prescribed time-limit. Every chess master moreover takes his vocation very seriously and he feels that each move is a contribution to his life's work. This may explain why most chess masters suffer a sort of nervous collapse after a mistake, especially after a game has been lost.

A stronger case for the existence of gamesmanship in chess is provided by instances where behaviour is deliberately altered in order to induce a state of mind in the opponent which causes him to lose his own objectivity. Take this piece of advice on endgame play offered by Belavenets and quoted by Kotov in *Think Like a Grandmaster* (1971):

> The basic rule of endgames is not to hurry. If you have a chance to advance a pawn one square or two, then first of all advance only one square, have a good look round, and only then play forward one more square. Repeating moves in an ending can be very useful. Apart from the obvious gain of time on the clock one notices that the side with the

> Fischer first wrote down the move 22 ♖a1-e1, without doubt the strongest, and wrote it not in his usual English notation but in European, almost Russian! And not very deftly he pushed the scoresheet towards me. 'He's asking me for an endorsement', I thought to myself, but how was I to react? To frown was impossible, if I smiled he would suspect trickery, and so I did the natural thing. I got up and began to walk calmly up and down the stage. I met Petrosian, made some joke with him and he replied. But the 15-year old Fischer . . . sat with a confused expression on his face . . .

Store your solution for the moment, and consider the next problem.
Suppose you are a Martian, and you want to find out whether the
following law is true false:

> *Anyone consuming alcohol on these premises must be at least eighteen*
> *years of age.*

Whom would you need to interrogate?

(i)   A person drinking whisky
(ii) A person drinking lemonade
(iii) A person over eighteen
(iv) A person under eighteen

The solution is (i), in order to establish the age, and (iv), in order to
establish the nature of the drink. But that problem has the identical
logical (or formal) structure to the one about letters and numbers –
its solution is also (i) and (iv).

The experimental facts are striking. Very few individuals get the
abstract problem right – they firmly adhere to the vowel and the even
number, or just the vowel. Second, many simply do not understand
the problem when it is explained to them. Third, and most important
in the present context, there is no 'transfer' between the familiar
drinking problem and the formally identical letters and numbers
problem. In other words, solving the familiar problem does not help
the individual to solve the abstract problem – indeed, many
individuals see no connection between the two. Exactly why this
should be so is still a highly controversial issue (Wason, 1983).

The parallel should be clear. The ability to play chess well may be
related to reasoning in a miniature universe which is highly
structured and over-learned, but not related to the world at large.
Recent research at the University of California at San Diego,
associated especially with the name of David Rumelhart, has related
this notion of context-dependent thinking (and it extends to
perception and memory for stories) to what is known as 'schema
theory'. This theory, which derives initially from Bartlett (1932),
is complex because it aims to cover a large variety of different
phenomena, but its postulation is necessary almost by default –
no other formulation of a more traditional kind can explain the
events in question. The theory assumes (i) that experience about the
world is stored in 'organized structures' in the brain; (ii) that these

structures can be triggered by the appropriate stimuli in such a way that elements within them can be mentally manipulated without conscious effort; and (iii) that the existence of structures of this kind accounts for a variety of implicit inferences which may, or may not, be correct. The power of the theory, or at least its plausibility, can be illustrated by a couple of examples. The following figurative passage may seem baffling (Dooling and Lachman, 1971):

> With hocked gems financing him our hero bravely defied all scornful laughter that tried to prevent his scheme. Your eyes deceive, he had said; an egg not a table correctly typifies this unexplored planet. Now, three sturdy sisters sought proof forging along sometimes through calm vastness yet more often over turbulent peaks and valleys. Days became weeks, as many doubters spread fearful rumours about the edge. At last from nowhere welcome winged creatures appeared signifying momentous success.

What is it all about? It might seem as devoid of meaning as a middle game position would be to a non-player. And yet the meaning of the passage becomes clear, but not through any process of calculation, when its title is supplied: *Christopher Columbus discovering America.* This is like a chess master unconsciously recognizing a chess pattern.

The second example concerns a peculiar sentence, first investigated by Wason and Reich (1979), which might be construed as a message to medical students:

> *No head injury is too trivial to be ignored*

Most individuals, confronted with this sentence, persist in thinking that it means that one must be very careful not to overlook head injuries however trivial they may appear. They remain unmoved by the consideration of the following sentence with the same syntax.

> *No guided missile is too small to be banned*

Since this sentence obviously means that every guided missile ought to be banned however small it may be, the former sentence obviously means that every head injury ought to be ignored however trivial it may be. Similarly, the sentence 'No WUG is too DAX to be ZONGED' ought to mean that every WUG should be ZONGED however DAX it may be. But these appeals to rationality (syntax) are rather like trying to justify a move in chess by exact calculation.

Since the head injury sentence is nonsensical (in different ways), its literal meaning is better evoked by associating it with a nonsensical 'schema':

> 'In our world', said the Red Queen to Alice, 'We make a special point of ignoring all head injuries – when I was your age I learned to ignore twenty a day'.
> 'Even the trivial ones?', murmured Alice.
> 'Of course, child', retorted the Red Queen, 'No head injury is too trivial to be ignored'.

Here schematic knowledge illuminates an absurd sentence in just the same way that the title illuminated the figurative prose passage. And in the same sort of way, we are inclined to think, the master is able to reconstruct a game position, after only seeing it for a few seconds, because of his vast store of schematic knowledge consisting of configurations of chess patterns. If this view is correct, it may mean that although playing chess at a rudimentary level may help people to think better, being very good at chess confers no extra benefits of a general kind at all. This, of course, does not in the least mean that excellence at chess should not be highly esteemed by the community. It affords, as we have seen, many kinds of satisfaction. It may be seen even to play a role in therapy because of its effect as an antidote to the aimless boredom which affects so much of modern existence (see Chapter 9).

One qualification is necessary to the important research described in this chapter. It seems to us that the theories associated with the board reconstruction experiments represent an idealized picture of master chess which may be misleading. Playing chess (at any level) is not just the cerebral activity of unconscious search, guided by 100,000 patterns in long-term memory. So often, as any player will agree, it is hopes and fears which seem to influence the choice of a move. Notoriously, the weaker player will tend to exaggerate both his advantages and his disadvantages, thinking he has a win with a good position, and a loss with a bad one. This emotional lability seems less obvious at higher levels. 'I have negative emotions about this game', said ex-World Champion Boris Spassky in a BBC World Cup Chess Tournament. He went on to win the game. At this level, the same emotions may be felt which beset the ordinary mortal, but they exert much less influence over the conduct of the game. A fault in a position may provide the spur for increased efforts rather than despair.

In this chapter we have described some of the research on the basic chess skill of seeing patterns, and mentally manipulating them to achieve a goal. The next chapter tries to assess the extent to which machines play good chess, and whether we can learn anything from their performance about how humans play chess.

6 Artificial Stupidity?

> The question is not merely whether a computer can be taught to play chess, but whether a computer can replace human perception to any great extent. If it is possible to arrive at an answer using chess as an example, a great contribution will have been made to the understanding of how the mind functions (Dr M.Euwe, 1970).

The idea of using computers to replace humans in areas of sophisticated decision-making is one which has been argued, at times with more emotion than logic, since the post-war beginnings of our modern technological era. For reasons easy to understand but hard to justify in a logical manner, the task of programming a computer to play good chess has assumed a high priority in the field which describes itself as Artificial Intelligence. The game has become the battlefield for a contest between human thought and computer power. The programmers seem to have lost sight of their original objective: that of simulating intelligent processes by mechanical means.

The question here is one of the meaning of intelligence. As we shall argue, human players approach chess in an intelligent manner. They make use of those facilities at which the brain is accomplished to approach a task for which it is objectively ill-designed. What is intelligent is the manner of tackling the problem. Even a bad player may play the game in an intelligent manner. The machine plays chess, generally speaking, in a totally different way. If it succeeds in producing better results than a human, that is no evidence of intelligence. If a computer played bad chess in the same way that a weak human player played, that would be a significant achievement in the programming of artificial intelligence. A subtle distinction might be made here between stupidity and mindlessness as terms of reprobation. We might define stupidity as an intelligent process gone haywire and mindlessness as an absence of any intelligence in the first place. On that basis, the bad chess produced by computers is, sadly, artificial mindlessness. Artificial stupidity, while producing no better results, would be on a higher plane of intelligent thought. We shall return to this topic later. First let us approach the problem of chess from the computer's point of view and take a look at just how they are programmed to play the game and to how great a degree that differs from the manner in which a human plays.

Naively, one might think that computers should play perfect chess. The game is finite, with a limited number of possibilities at each move and an upper bound on the length of the game. A sufficiently fast machine ought to be able to work it all out, just by analysing any given position, through to mate or a draw. A quick calculation, however, shows that this approach is wildly over-optimistic. Computers can indeed cope with large numbers of calculations in a short time, but the numbers involved in chess quickly become too vast. As a crude guide to computing speeds, it is reasonable to suppose that tens of millions of operations might be coped with, but once the numbers become hundreds or thousands of millions then they begin to feel the strain. In an average chess position there are around thirty possible moves. One White move followed by a Black reply therefore can lead to about 900 possibilities. By the time we have counted the options in analysing three full moves deep, we are already close to that figure of a thousand million ramifications. And most chess positions will admit far longer variations which must be considered even before a superficial judgment can be reached. So the machine must employ some selectivity in its thoughts. It cannot look at everything. The programmer's first task is to introduce some means of limiting those variations considered. He has to give the machine some idea of what a good move looks like. The human player, thanks to his experience of the game, develops an almost intuitive feel for a promising move. This helps to limit calculations to a few hundred possibilities.

Several studies, notably those of de Groot, have suggested that any player's thoughts will only encompass such a relatively small number of different positions. The difference between stronger and weaker players is in the ability to detect which are the relevant positions for consideration. One reason, of course, that human players do limit their considerations to so few of the possible continuations is that any significantly greater number would tend to confuse rather than enlighten the overloaded mind. The computer has nothing to correspond with human intuition, the chess player's ability to zero in on the important features of a position, but it has the compensating advantage of enormous speed. In the same time that the human looks at two hundred positions, making his judgments, the machine will have looked at as many as two million. In those two million, therefore, can be included a large amount of relative junk in the hope that the computer's huge net will ensnare everything thought of by the comparatively easily confused human mind. The temptation to make full use of this enormous calculating ability has proven too hard for most chess programmers to resist. And those who have resisted, abandoning the brute force method in favour of continuing to attempt a close simulation of human thought processes, have been less successful in what is now the primary goal of producing good chess from a computer. Let us examine the 'thought processes' of a typical chess computer. As we shall see, it is a very different animal from the human player, with distinct strengths and weaknesses. An examination of such mechanical models can give us further insights into the way the human mind tackles the problem of chess.

After the computer has been taught to recognise legal moves (a tedious but inherently trivial part of the programmer's task) it needs to be given an algorithm with which to select its moves. The digital computer can only 'think' in terms of numerical values, so at the core of its chess understanding must lie a Positional Evaluation Function, a system of assigning numerical values to the features of a position and combining them in a manner which indicates who stands better and by how much. A sophisticated Evaluation Function is essential to any effective program. It must take into account as many as possible of the positional features which a human player would consider important in forming his judgment of the position. To this end numerical values must be assigned to such features as material, control of the centre, control of the rest of the board, attacking possibilities, king safety, pawn structure, piece mobility and so on. Any position can then be assessed by the Positional Evaluation Function to arrive at a figure indicating whether White or Black scores more highly. The next stage in the procedure is to decide which positions should be assessed in this manner: the machine must build its Tree of Analysis.

Certain moves must be analysed: captures, mate threats and

checks have to be given priority treatment. Also attacks on large pieces by smaller pieces or pawns deserve attention. In general, any move which limits the opponent's choice of reply ought to be looked at first. These introduce the forcing lines of play which may be susceptible to precise analysis. Any string of captures, for example, must necessarily terminate, so the machine can be instructed to look at all such sequences. A simple piece count will then determine whether material can be gained by such a continuation. While humans can blunder pieces away by miscalculations of order or number of captures, a machine ought never to do so. Besides the forcing variations, which have to be looked at, the Tree of Analysis will usually grow other branches to see what might lie ahead. Typically, the tree might start with seven moves indicated as potentially fruitful by the Positional Evaluation Function, those moves which, without analysing possible replies, appear to improve the position most. The seven most promising replies for the opponent may be selected for each of these candidate moves. The process may be continued until the analysis has reached, say, the machine's fourth move. To continue this far (i.e. seven half-moves deep) would give 7^7 possible paths in the tree, which is still less than one million, so we might hope that it is within the capacity of the machine. At the end of the chosen depth of analysis, all the final positions may be assessed again by the Evaluation Function and on this basis a move may be selected which guarantees the best prospects.

Though considerably simplified, that is essentially how nearly all chess programs are designed. Much time can be saved in calculation by efficient 'tree-pruning' techniques whereby irrelevant branches of the tree may be lopped off and ignored. Many branches will never need to be inspected at all once other paths are found promising richer pickings. (When you have found a good move look for a better one, don't waste time on worse ones!) However efficient the pruning-shears, the Tree of Analysis and the Positional Evaluation Function are the main factors in the success or failure of any chess program. Growing the right tree and assessing the positions accurately are the main tasks for the programmer. Let us consider some of the typical problems which face him. The drawbacks of machine chess can be summarised under three broad headings:

1 When the analysis has to stop

The direct calculation of forced variations ought to be what the computer does best. And so it is, but there remain severe problems even in this area of computer chess thought. What is required is a workable and effective rule for deciding when a line of analysis has proceeded sufficiently deeply to be considered terminated. A fixed depth of search is clearly inadequate. One might easily stop in the middle of a series of captures, or the next move could be checkmate. A human analyst will develop a keen sense of when to stop analysing; he knows when there are still things going on in the position which have to be pursued further. The machine suffers from 'horizon effect', a short-sightedness which prevents it from looking any further than decreed by its program. The difficulty lies in an effective definition of quiescence, the state in which nothing tactically important is happening. Analysis of forced variations stops when the position is quiescent, but a mechanical definition of that state is hard to find which preserves the Tree of Analysis at a manageable yet effective size.

Two simple examples show the type of problem which poses a major difficulty for the machine-type intelligence, yet can be simple for an experienced human. With White to move in this position there is a clearly forcing continuation in 1 ♕xf6 gf. There are no more captures, checks or mate threats, but is this the right moment to stop analysing and assess the position on purely static positional grounds? It is not; for the human player will realise immediately that 2 a4 will force the promotion of the white pawn. The analysis must proceed until White's sixth move (2 a4 ♚f8 3 a5 ♚e8 4 a6 ♚d8 5 a7 ♚c8 6 a8♕) to confirm this fact. How does the machine know that it must look a further five moves after the exchange of queens when, by most normal criteria, the position is quiescent? We can see another typical symptom of the horizon effect if we imagine that by some chance our machine is programmed to look exactly six moves ahead. Would it not then find that White wins with 1 ♕xf6? The chances are that it would not. An exhaustive search would unearth the variation 1 ♕xf6 gf 2 a4 h5 3 a5 h4 4 a6 h3 5 a7 h2+ 6 ♔xh2. Still the white pawn has not reached the queening square and the analysis stops because move six is reached. What the machine has done is to postpone the crucial move (a8♕) until it is over the edge of the horizon. As far as it is concerned, Black's problems are over. In fact, one can imagine such a computer playing the move 1 ♕xf6 in this position for the simple reason that it wins a pawn (6 ♔xh2!) rather than for the more convincing reason that the white a-pawn cannot be stopped at all.

Of course, one may incorporate into a program an instruction to look for passed pawns and see if they can be stopped, but even such a simple sounding order is difficult to make rigorous. Sequences of captures may always be pursued to an end, since each capture diminishes the number of pieces on the board. A string of captures must therefore terminate, and usually does so quickly. Equally, the board may be examined for any mating move. The task is therefore comparatively easy to ensure that the computer misses no chance to mate on the move, or win material by captures, or give checkmate within a capturing sequence. Once we progress into even slightly more complicated tactics, the job becomes much harder. Here is a simple opening position to illustrate a typical problem.

Most players will recognise a common tactical theme here: 1 ♘xe5 ♘xe5 2 d4 and White regains his piece. Leaving aside the job of assessing the positional merits of the whole idea (i.e. an assessment of the position after the dust has settled) let us consider what type of instruction the machine must be given to be able to 'see' such a possibility. How is it to know that it should look further after apparent quiescence is reached with 1 ♘xe5 ♘xe5? All one can say is that sequences of captures ought always to proceed one half-move (one White move or one Black move) further than the last capture to discover if any gains of material can be forced which will affect our judgment of the position. To be quite certain we would have to permit the inclusion into the capturing sequence of any heavy threats which can be made at any time. But the introduction of non-capturing moves into our tree of forcing variations brings with it an end to the guarantee that branches will terminate within a reasonable number of moves, or indeed that they will terminate at all. Such daft lines as 1 ♘xe5 ♘xe5 2 d4 ♕h4 3 dc ♘g4 4 g3, or 1 ♘xe5 ♘xe5 2 d4 d5 3 dc ♗g4 have to be considered and pursued to their conclusions before true quiescence is reached. A further insight into the nature of the problem is revealed if we move the white pawn from g2 to g3 in the original position. Then the whole idea is incorrect since 1 ♘xe5 ♘xe5 2 d4 ♗xd4 3 ♕xd4 ♘f3+ loses White his queen, but how does the machine know that it must look beyond 3 ♕xd4? What is for the human a simple process of identifying the important variations worth calculating is, for the computer, largely a matter of stumbling about seeing what might turn up. Of course, any good tactical program would certainly find that 1 ♘xe5 is indeed tactically correct with the pawn on g2 and incorrect with the pawn on g3, but the mass of variations examined to establish those conclusions would bear no relation to the concise and direct analysis a human player would make to reach the same conclusion. When the machine enters the realms of long, complex tactical calculations with threats, counter-threats, captures and checks all combined, it is hard to conceive of a when-to-stop rule which will both include all that is important and avoid analysing so much that it becomes unwieldy.

2 Quantitative positional assessment

The digital computer is by nature a numerical beast. Its calculations arrive at a figure (or a set of figures) which evaluate the position. It will declare that White has an advantage of +125 or a disadvantage standing at –137 for example. A move which guarantees an advantage of +125 whatever the opponent does, will be preferred to a move which can only promise +83. But chess is about winning and losing. At some stage in the game, one side's advantage turns into a winning position, after which even the best moves cannot save the opponent. Any disadvantage may be tolerated so long as it is not bad enough to result inexorably in a loss. A cramped position, for example, may be considered unpleasant and demanding precise defensive play, but need not be fatal. The human player has to develop a very fine sense of the tolerable levels of weakness of chess positions. A good defensive player will hold his inferior positions at the level usually described as 'difficult' without letting them be pushed over the threshold of hopelessness. The problem for a computer is to define this threshold so that it may be recognised numerically. Most noticeably in endgames, the difference between a winning position and a drawn one can be so slight that only a long and precise analysis of the position can detect it. As the position simplifies, the human player switches from an assessment based on nuances of advantage and disadvantage into a concrete assessment of win, draw or loss. Returning to the diagram on page 69, we might imagine that the queen and pawn endgame has been proceeding for some time with White suffering under a large disadvantage. If it is Black's move now, he must somehow know that 1 ... ♛xf2+ 2 ♚xf2 leads to a position which can be evaluated precisely as win, loss or draw. In fact it is a win for Black (2 ... ♚f8! or 2 ... ♚f7!) but if his king were on h8 at the start, Black would lose. The problem of transition from an advantageous middle game into an endgame is, for the human player, very often a question of whether he is certain that he will win the endgame. He knows that he has the advantage in the middle game, but he is in the process of giving up his +127 (or whatever it may be in machine terms) for a more brutal 1, ½ or perhaps 0. How can a machine recognise when the moment has come to switch from a continuous quantitative assessment to a win/loss/draw scheme? Arbitrary cut-off points, however well chosen, simply cannot work. No positional assessment can be so sensitive that +200, say, will always be a winning position when +199 will only be enough to draw.

Recognition of the moment when a position turns from 'difficult' to 'lost' is only one of the defects of single-figure positional assessment functions. Although adding together one's advantages and subtracting the disadvantages is a convenient means of arriving at an overall assessment, it does not correspond well with the way a human player thinks. In particular a strong player will recognise the difference in importance between static and dynamic features of a position. The static features are important in forming positional judgments which will determine long-term strategy; the dynamic features involve precise calculation and may lead to further long-term gains or losses. The calculation of the dynamics and the judgment of the statics take their places on different levels of the decision-making process. One cannot simply add one to the other.

3   Trees grow upwards

The computer Tree of Analysis relies on a simple growth pattern, starting at move one and working forward, taking plausible looking moves at each stage and continuing for some time before finally seeing what has been achieved at the designated end. This is again very different from the human approach which proceeds in a more constructive process of self-inquisition. What's going on in this position? What should I be trying to do? How do I get there from here? While the human is forming his sub-goals, the computer lurches forward, kicking hard and scoring what goals might accidentally happen. Here is a simple example of a human thought process which would be inconceivable for a machine: White's

elementary endgame knowledge would tell him that he cannot win by kingside play alone. He formulates the plan of abandoning the f-pawn and racing to the queenside. The first variation examined might be 1 ♔e4 ♔f7 2 ♔d5 ♔f6 3 ♔c6 ♔xf5 4 ♔b6 ♔e6 5 ♔xa6 ♔d7 6 ♔b7! and the a-pawn queens. How can Black avoid this variation? It is simple (for the human player) to realise that the only possibly significant manner in which Black can alter this variation is by ensuring that his pawn is captured on a different square. So the next variation looks less promising for White: 1 ♔e4 a5! 2 ♔f4 ♔f7 3 ♔e5 ♔e7 4 ♔d5 ♔f6 5 ♔c6 ♔xf5 6 ♔b6 ♔e6 7 ♔xa5 ♔d7 8 ♔b6 ♔c8 and Black draws. Finally, White will realise that the correct move (and the only one to win) is 1 a5! fixing the pawn on a6 and ensuring its capture on that square. Equally, if Black has the move in the starting position 1 ... a5! is the only move to draw. A human player realises easily that the only important factor is the square on which Black's pawn is captured, but a mechanistic process of analysis, starting at move one and stumbling forward, has no procedure within which to reach that type of conclusion.

To be fair to machines, there are programs written specifically for king and pawn endgames which would have a chance of finding the right move, for the right reasons, in such a position. But king and pawn endings are only a small part of chess and most of the 'general principles' which are specific to such endings have no place in an algorithm for other types of position. The idea has been suggested that a computer might be developed with several different programs, for king and pawn, knight and pawn, rook and pawn endgames, for middle game attacks, blocked positions, different openings etc, letting the machine select the appropriate program for the type of position it was in and changing as the game progressed. Such an approach is hardly credible. As strong players realise, there is nothing inherently different about the various phases of the game. The important fact is that some positions allow more detailed and precise analysis than others. Just as a sub-goal may be formulated in an endgame (let's rush to the queenside and get his a-pawn), so may a strategic sub-goal be formulated and carried out in a middle game (I'll try to advance the kingside pawns and open a file to give attacking prospects). The human approach – look at the position and see what one ought to be trying to do – is radically different from the machine's line of attack – look at the available moves and see what they accomplish. There is, incidentally, no objective proof that the human method is necessarily a superior approach. It is certainly more suited to the human's limited potential for tree-growing.

Leaving aside for the moment the mechanical processes of computer thought, let us see how a human player utilises his thinking resources to deal with with the problem of selecting chess moves. While the computer relies on precision and intensity of calculation, the human has a well-developed skill of pattern recognition as his greatest asset. A strong player's experience is the key to his understanding. Rather than calculate the consequences of available moves, he uses his experience of similar positions to select appropriate piece and pawn formations. As de Groot's position reconstruction task shows, he sees the pieces not as single entities, but as recognisable groups of co-operating units. He compares the position with others encountered previously and notes the points of similarity and difference. Faced with an unfamiliar middle game position, any strong player ought to be able to identify correctly the opening variation which was adopted and to sketch the past history of the game. He could then go on to enumerate the possible plans for both sides and suggest the thematic moves for conducting the play in the near future.

There is a strong analogy between the acquisition of chess ability and the learning of language. As we saw in Chapter 5, experiments have suggested that the number of groups of chessmen which a master can recognise at a glance is around 100,000. That is the same order of magnitude as the number of words in a natural language. It has been suggested that the chess player acquires this 'vocabulary' in the same way as language is acquired, and in about the same length of time. A chess position is thus perceived as a collection of 'words', each word being a group of pieces in an instantly recognisable pattern (though the same piece may feature in more than one word). The whole position is a sentence (or even a paragraph) of which the meaning is clear to the chess-fluent player. The tactics of chess are analogous to the grammar of the language. Tactically incorrect moves may be thought of as producing grammatical errors. At a higher level of chess thought, tactically correct moves produce meaningful sentences expressing strategic ideas. The chess player's task is to work out the complex syntax of the sentences on the board. While language was designed by the human brain for its own use, chess may be an example of our using closely related skills for a totally different task.

As with any analogy, this can easily be pursued too far, but it is probably fair to say that in chess as in language the difference between the master and the amateur is that one is concerned with the expression of profound ideas, whereas the other is still struggling to avoid breaking the grammatical rules. For a computer the avoidance of grammatical mistakes in both chess and language is a relatively simple task. Producing good prose is quite another matter.

A characteristically human chess process is to think in terms of plans. He decides what he should be trying to do and where he would like his pieces to stand in a few moves time. Then he attempts to set them on course for their destinations. Each move is another brick in the grand design, which is itself undergoing constant modifications as the position changes and new priorities emerge. Whether this is the way chess ought to be played is an interesting question for chess philosophers. The computer's method might be considered preferable on the grounds that it tends to treat each position as a new task to find the best move, irrespective of the past history of the game which led to that position. A player's choice of move will often be influenced by what has happened previously in the game, though objectively that should be irrelevant to the thought process. Many instances may be cited of players overlooking strong moves simply because those moves do not play a part in their grand design for the game. Tactical opportunism operates on a different level from strategic planning.

Perhaps the human's greatest asset is the ability to indulge in two distinct types of chess calculation: precise analysis and 'fuzzy' analysis. Precise analysis is the calculation of forced variations. Just as the computer must consider captures, checks and heavy threats, the same applies to a human player. The possible forced lines of play must be resolved before any architect's plans are drawn up for the grand strategic plan. Having disposed of these precise calculations, the thinking becomes fuzzy. The player feels his way forward to see how the position is likely to develop within the next few moves. Generally this fuzzy thought will proceed to a depth of four or five moves until the player feels comfortable with his position. No definite conclusions are reached beyond a feeling of preference for a particular move. Whereas the precise calculations must proceed along all paths until quiescence is reached, the fuzzy thought just wanders along paths directed by the strategic plan until the player is happy with the outcome (or at least until he has come to terms with his confusion).

This whole procedure can be described as an hierarchical structure in the thought processes. At the lowest level lies the precise tactical calculation of forcing variations; at the top level, strategic judgment takes its overview. In between the fuzzy thought translates strategic plans into single moves. A player's thoughts will constantly jump from level to level. The highest (strategic) level suggests desirable moves, which may introduce new tactics needing to be referred downstairs for sorting out tactically. When that is done, the analysis can proceed at the middle level. Each time a line of analysis comes to an end, it has to be referred again to the top level for judgment. Under this scheme, the strategic level is analogous to the computer's

Positional Evaluation Function. The tactical analysis forms a large part of its Tree of Analysis. What the machine cannot successfully simulate is the groping process of fuzzy thought by which a player decides on the method of implementation of a known strategic plan.

More precisely, the human method of chess thought puts heavy emphasis on pattern recognition. His experience of past games, both played and read, is processed in a manner which leads to the formulation of chess concepts. The brain's ability to recognise patterns operates on a scarcely conscious level to identify the useful words in the chess language. Faced with a new position its relevant features may be detected from the player's ever developing library of chess heuristics.

The philosopher Roland Puccetti, in a provocative paper entitled 'Pattern Recognition in Computers and the Human Brain: With Special Application to Chess Playing Machines' (1974), suggests fundamental limitations in the ability of digital computers to simulate human thought. He argues that the modes of thought of the two halves of the brain are distinct. The left cerebral hemisphere in right-handed adults controls language and appears to face insurmountable difficulties when posed tasks of which the manner of solution does not admit a verbal description. Pattern recognition is the domain of the right side of the brain. Such complex tasks as recognition of human faces may be performed with ease by this hemisphere, though the left brain is unable to explain in words the process of recognition. Puccetti's argument is that digital computers may be able to simulate the processes of the left brain, but the visual-spatial abilities of the right brain cannot be reproduced by mechanical means. His conclusions are supported by Zobrist and Carlson writing about an advice-taking chess computer in *Scientific American* in 1973:

> It is possible that a significant portion of human chess technique cannot be expressed in words. For example, a grandmaster might be quite unable to explain the reasoning behind a particularly brilliant move. It is not just a question of whether one can have thoughts without words but of whether one can have thoughts of much greater content than the words one can find to express them. It is possible that chess thought depends heavily on spatial perception and that the perceptual processes involved are so subtle and rapid that only the final outcome reaches conscious expression. If so, there may be no adequate language for conveying chess knowledge to a computer.

Puccetti speculates on the possibility of a chess game played between the two halves of a person's brain. He even explains how one might set up such a match after the operation severing connections between the hemispheres. 'The really interesting question is whether the speech hemisphere, left to its own resources, has the means of visually processing significant chess patterns, and thus putting up a good fight'. Experience with chess computers strongly suggests that humans rely on their right-brain for information processing and planning, otherwise one might suppose that computers would play better than they do. But perhaps left on its own, the right-brain would be too blunder-prone and be outplayed by the naive calculations of the left.

The attempts to write computer programs to play good chess rely heavily on what a computer is good at: the processing of vast amounts of data at enormous speed. By looking at millions of possible continuations the machine hopes, by a process of overkill, to include all that a good player would look at. One of the human skills which seems beyond the machine is an excellent feeling for what is irrelevant; only this enables our thoughts to be kept within manageable limits. Why then have not attempts been made to write programs based more closely on human thought processes? The answer is that such attempts have been made, but have generally been abandoned through lack of success. Even if one manages to define and separate the levels of hierarchical thought, the most difficult task is finding an effective means of communication between the levels of the hierarchy. As many programmers have found, it is no easy feat to integrate tactical analysis and strategic planning in a manner which preserves their separate functions.

In the world of computer chess, brute force rules. And this is a pity, because it offers little prospect of our learning anything valuable about the human thought processes. If computers, using present methods, do finally manage to play better chess than the best human players, this would tell us something about chess but little about our mode of thinking. Machines already play top-class draughts and backgammon. Indeed it was a consideration of the reasons for the difficulties behind computer chess programs which led Hans Berliner towards his successful backgammon program. Perhaps when the fastest computers can look at four million positions each move, they will finally solve the problem of chess, but the economy of thought of the human chess mind will remain impressive by comparison.

Alan Turing (1950) proposed a famous test to answer the question, 'Can machines think?'. An interrogator asks questions to a computer in one room and a man in another. The answers come back to him on a teleprinter. His task is to identify which room contains the computer and which the human. If a machine can be programmed to disguise its true identity in this manner then we might say that it can indeed think. It would be interesting to formulate an analogous test for chess computers. More interesting than the question of whether computers can play better than humans is the question of whether one could be programmed to play in a manner similar to that of humans. Would a human player always be able to identify whether he was facing another man or a machine? In some recent simultaneous displays in West Germany, boards have been taken by people making the moves, communicated in secret, suggested by a computer. After the displays the grandmasters were told that they had faced a computer on one board and invited to guess which. In most cases they have failed to do so. While quite impressive, that is not a completely fair method of conducting the chess Turing test. The grandmaster's task was simply to win all his games. Had he been concerned primarily with determining which was the machine, without caring about the result of the games, his play would have been different.

We would propose that a test be conducted in the following manner: a strong chess player sits in one room, posing chess positions to a computer and a human in another room. The human may be of any chess strength, though some experience of the game would be desirable. Both communicate their replies to the interrogator. Can a program be written in such a manner that the strong player would be unable to distinguish between the two respondents? Even if one could produce a program which simulated the thoughts of a very weak player, it would be a considerable achievement in artificial intelligence.

Let us finish on a more optimistic note for the computers. The position overleaf was recently submitted to one of the strongest available microprocessors. It found the solution (1 ♖f8+ ♔xf8 2 ♕h8+ ♔f7 3 ♖f1+ ♔g6 4 ♕h5 mate) in less than a minute, as indeed might have been expected since the whole variation is totally forced. Let us amend the position slightly be moving the pawn on g4 back to g3. This becomes a far harder task both for machine and man. A human who had just solved the previous task, or indeed

White to Play

had encountered something similar to its final mating position before, ought eventually to find the solution: 1 ♖f8+ ♚xf8 2 ♕h8+ ♚f7 3 ♖f1+ ♚g6 4 g4! and Black can do nothing to prevent 5 ♕h5 mate. But White's fourth move is non-forcing; Black has a large number of possible replies, none any use whatsoever. For a machine, it is hard to conceive of the possibility that the position after 3 ... ♚g6 is not quiescent and that it is worth looking further. The microprocessor found the solution after forty minutes' thought. The curious point is that if a human player had thought for so long about the position, one would have expected him to miss the winning combination (assuming he met the task in a real game rather than as an artificial White-to-play-and-win problem). The search for a forced win occupies the front end of a human player's thoughts. Once the forcing variations have been abandoned, it is unlikely he will return to find the answer. But that is a human weakness a computer would find very hard to simulate.

7 Subjectivity

Are the cogitations of chess players the cool, calm and objective procedures we are led to believe? A purely abstract consideration of the game could lead to the conclusion that the selection of a move ought to be a purely logical process. The player must make certain judgments about the state of play on the board, he must calculate a number of possible continuations, and finally, on the basis of these calculations, select the best move. But life on the chess board is rarely so simple. Subjective considerations are not only a common feature of a chess master's thought processes but even form an essential part of the decision-making procedure.

In some chess positions a thorough analysis may demonstrate that there is one and only one best move. Perhaps it is the only move leading to a forced win, or the only move to save the game when all others lose, or even the only move to continue the struggle when alternatives lead to a demonstrable loss. In general, however, this is not the case. Most positions offer more than one acceptable move. If that were not so, there would be no room for style in chess. In most positions purely logical considerations will lead at best to a short list of possibilities; after that the choice is a matter of personal predilection, which may even be influenced by subjective criteria far removed from the chessboard. As we shall see, these subjective considerations may even induce a player, for good or ill, to select a move which logical analysis has already eliminated from the short list of candidates.

The task of a chess player is twofold: to avoid errors himself, and to induce errors from the opponent. No game can be lost without a mistake nor any win achieved without some help from the opponent. Some players concentrate their efforts largely on the avoidance of errors. Ensuring themselves against defeat in this manner, they rely on unprovoked mistakes from the other side of the board to provide their victories. Those players who consciously adopt a policy of risky play in order to tempt errors from their opponents are indulging a higher proportion of subjectivity in their play. The fundamental question is whether one is playing the man or the board. To what extent should one be consciously trying to take advantage of the opponent's fallibility and to what degree should a player tailor his moves to fit an individual opponent? These questions will be answered in very different fashion by players of distinct temperaments. When Akiba Rubinstein was once asked who his opponent was to be in the next round of a tournament, he replied: 'That is not important. Today I play against the black pieces' (Krogius, 1981). Compare this attitude with Richard Réti's (1923) diagnosis of the secret behind Emanuel Lasker's success:

> For him the essential element is this contest of the nerves; he uses the medium of the chess game to fight above all his opponent's psyche, and he knows how to bring about the nervous collapse, which otherwise occurs only after a mistake, even before a mistake has happened, and to make this the very cause of subsequent errors . . . He is not so much interested in making the objectively best moves as those most disagreeable to his opponent; he turns the game in a direction not suitable to the style of his opponent and on this unaccustomed road leads him to the abyss, often by means of intentionally bad moves . . .

Dr Tartakower was the first to point out that one can win games not only by the opponent's mistakes, but also by one's own. The willingness to play an objectively inferior move and accept a difficult position can, in suitable circumstances, place the opponent under stress. Mikhail Tal gives a good example of this in his disarmingly honest account of the 1960 World Championship match. His move 12 f4 in the seventeenth game against Botvinnik was a strategic monstrosity, compromising his position for no reason other than to avoid a dead equality.

> At first I felt rather awkward . . . The advantages of this move are less obvious, but they are there nonetheless, even though they may lie outside the realm of the 64 squares on the chessboard. First of all, this move will have to be refuted, which should entail the possibility of a double-edged struggle, which, judging from M.Botvinnik's style of play in this match, would not be desirable for him.

In the ensuing complications Botvinnik lost his way in time trouble and Tal won the game. Tal's explanation of his success was simple: ' . . . he succeeded in proving that it was risky but at the cost of nervous tension which turned out to be too great' (Tal, 1977).

At an earlier stage of his career Tal admits to facing difficulties in learning to win games at decisive moments of tournaments or matches. He writes: 'Later . . . I began to succeed in decisive games. Perhaps because I realised a very simple truth: not only was I worried, but also my opponent'. Such a realisation is the key to understanding how to cope with the nervous tension in a chess game. Absorbed in their own anxieties, many players will easily forget that the opponent has problems too. The tension in a chess game is created not only by the intense level of concentration necessary to keep clear sight of one's calculations, but perhaps more so by the struggle of nerves between the two contestants. Back to Réti (1923) again:

> Every game of chess in a way is a contest of the nerves. Tournament play is essentially different from work in the quiet of one's own study, where you work when you feel so disposed and where you rest when you are tired; it is a relentless intellectual struggle before a numerous public, at a prescribed hour and with a prescribed time-limit. Every chess master moreover takes his vocation very seriously and he feels that each move is a contribution to his life's work. This may explain why most chess masters suffer a sort of nervous collapse after a mistake, especially after a game has been lost.

The importance of a sound nervous disposition to a chess master cannot be overestimated. Of Rubinstein, Réti writes: ' . . . has created the most perfect games of the epoch . . . truly great abilities . . . These victories Rubinstein was able to win in spite of the fact that there is scarcely another master who suffers so from nerves, which cause him moments of complete exhaustion, when he commits crude blunders'. It is no surprise that this description is of the man whom we have already met as the opponent not of another master but of 'the black pieces'. As an academic, white-versus-black chess player Rubinstein had no peers, but he shied away from the competitive fight.

We should mention here the subject of luck in chess, which bears a strong relationship to the degree of subjectivity of a player's thought processes. Generally the players who have acquired a reputation for luck are those whose styles have had a strong subjective component. Réti on Lasker again:

In analysing Lasker's tournament games I was struck by his lasting and at first seemingly incredible good luck. There are tournaments in which he came out on top and won almost every game, though in a losing position in every other game, so that many masters spoke of Lasker's hypnotic influence over his opponents. What is the truth? Again and again I studied Lasker's games to discover the secret of his success. There is no denying the fact that over and over again Lasker's lay-out of the game is poor, that he is in a losing position a hundred times and nevertheless wins in the end. The hypothesis of lasting luck is too improbable. A man who steadily wins such success must be possessed of surprising power. But why then the bad, the losing positions? There is only one answer, which may sound paradoxical at first blush: Lasker often deliberately plays badly.

Réti returns to the theme of encouraging one's own luck when he comes later in *Masters of the Chessboard* (1932) to discuss another of his greatest contemporaries:

It is well known that Bogoljubow, just like Lasker, is one of those chess masters who have had exceptionally good luck. This luck is not undeserved, however, but a consequence of the method of play. Most chess players in a poor position make the mistake of attacking impetuously, at all costs, and without regard for the positional requirements of the situation. The usual result is that they lose still more quickly. To understand this, it is necessary to imagine the psychology of the player who finds that he has the advantage. His chief and anxious concern will be to make sure of what he has won, to avoid traps, to simplify matters, in short and above all to defend. Thus it is natural that desperate attacks on the part of his opponent will almost always fail. In order to play correctly in poor positions, one must recognise and turn to account the psychological weaknesses of the player who has the advantage. This weakness consists in that very fact that he wants to avoid complications and combinations, that he would like to win in a simple manner, without undertaking any new attacks, and especially without making any sacrifices.

Accordingly, the psychologically correct procedure for a player who finds himself in a bad position is as follows: he must strengthen to the utmost possible extent such strong points and lines to which he is positionally entitled to lay claim, so that his opponent, who has relaxed his efforts and hopes to win without further struggle, finds real obstacles in his path which cannot easily be overcome.

We have quoted at length from Réti not only for the accuracy and pertinence of his comments, but as a rare example of a great player's eloquent exposition of a style of chess quite alien to his own. The 'lucky' style, if we may call it so, may be summarised as the willingness to compromise one's own position in order to upset the emotional equilibrium of the opponent. By raising his hopes then introducing a series of unexpected obstacles, one may hope to induce nervousness and errors. Resolute defence can win a game just as surely as forthright attack. The danger of such a style, of course, is that it can all too easily be carried too far. What is needed is a very precise feeling for the difference between a difficult position and a lost position. Difficult positions may be accepted, with confidence in one's ability to defend them accurately, but deliberately courting a lost position places too much reliance on the opponent's fallibility.

There are, therefore, broadly speaking two styles of player: those willing to take risks in order to persuade their opponents to make mistakes, and those who will do everything to reduce their own likelihood of errors. Which style an individual player adopts is a function of his willingness to live dangerously on the chessboard, his willingness to accept the risk of the pain of defeat. Curiously, personal animosity towards an opponent appears to have little influence in this decision. Mikhail Tal (1976) writes: 'Neither Spassky nor I have the slightest desire to play against opponents for whom we have a feeling of enmity, whereas Botvinnik and Korchnoi try to arouse such a feeling in themselves before a game'. Yet of those four names, one would ally Tal with Korchnoi as risk-takers and Botvinnik with Spassky as chess purists. Presumably while personal enmity for an opponent can heighten the emotions of victory, it would also make defeat more bitter.

Besides the willingness to accept risk, there are many other non-objective criteria which may influence a player's choice of move. Most players will alter their style to suit different opponents. Even the simple fact of whether an opponent is considered stronger or weaker than oneself can have an important bearing on one's optimism and the way one handles the game. Hugh Alexander was certainly not in the least overawed by the prestige of an opponent, and yet he provides us with a good example of the initial impact of a stronger player as soon as the game starts:

> If you play Botvinnik, it is even alarming to see him write his move down. Slightly short-sighted, he stoops over his scoresheet and devotes his entire attention to recording the move in the most beautifully clear script; one feels that an explosion would not distract him and that examined through a microscope not an irregularity would appear. When he wrote down 1. c2-c4 against me, I felt like resigning. (1973)

On a more systematic level, a study of the opponent's games, especially in match play, can reveal his strategic likes and dislikes. Most players concentrate on trying to reach positions in which they feel comfortable, but an equally effective procedure, especially against players of limited style, is to head for positions in which they do not feel at home. Writing of his preparations for the 1960 World Championship match with Botvinnik, Tal (1977) identified his opponent's strengths as follows:

> ... harmony of logical conceptions, strict consistency in realization of a plan and the skill to impose his style of play on his opponent. During the game he gives most of his consideration to strategic questions, not being distracted by difficult tactical variations. He is less sure of himself when caught in a combinational storm.

This suited Tal well, who brewed up storm clouds to great effect. Unfortunately for him, in the return match the following year Botvinnik did indeed impose his style of play on his opponent.

Taking the opponent into account, even to the extent of taking risks which are hard to justify on logical grounds, might be considered part of a legitimate, objective thought process. After all, even a game such as poker subscribes to the laws of probability and logic. And one can certainly bluff in poker. In chess too a certain amount of bluffing can be no bad thing.

We have considered so far mainly the positive aspects of subjectivity, but other non-objective factors can have a harmful effect on the quality of move finally chosen. We shall come to the psychology of blunders in a moment. Before that, however, we should mention a factor which seems commonly to cloud the thought processes.

Ideally, a game of chess could be seen as a series of isolated decisions by a player, each move of the game being his solution to the task of finding the best move in the position in front of him. To approach and solve this task, he does not need to know the past history of the game, or even the opponent's previous move. Each position may be assessed anew, the strategically appropriate plan decided, calculations made and a move produced. In practice, however, considerable effort is saved by remembering what was passing through one's mind on the previous move. The board is seen as a continuously changing landscape, each move modifying one's view. It is a common fault to fail to keep pace with the changing scenery and play a move which is no longer appropriate to the position. Perhaps more commonly still, one's emotions may fail to keep up with the game. Playing for a win when it is no longer justified, or missing a fleeting winning chance during a period of dour defence, are mistakes we have all made. The past history of the game, or even the recent history of one's own thoughts and emotions in thinking about a single move, can have undesirable consequences in polluting the purity of one's thought processes. The following two examples are both from Tal's games. His annotations are full of the honest introspection which is so revealing and so rare.

Firstly, writing about the fourth game of his 1968 Candidates match with Larsen, Tal (1976) confesses surprise after the moves 1 e4 ♘f6 2 e5 ♘d5 3 d4 d6 4 ♘f3 de 5 ♘xe5 when Larsen played 5 ... ♘d7. He spent nearly an hour in thought calculating the variations which could follow the piece sacrifice 6 ♘xf7 ♔xf7 7 ♕h5+ ♔e6. Intuitively he believed that the sacrifice must be correct, but he knew that Larsen must have analysed it. Finally he convinced himself that Black could defend. He refrained from making the sacrifice, but he could not remove it from his mind:

> Even after I had gained the advantage, my thoughts kept returning to the critical position. And somewhere in the middle of the game I suddenly came to the conclusion that in one variation which I had examined and thought to be in Black's favour, White could in fact obtain a decisive advantage. This I could not endure and I played the second half of the game aimlessly.

Even two weeks later that same position influenced his decision in the decisive last game of the match. Another opportunity presented itself to play a promising piece sacrifice. Again Tal was unsure whether he ought to take the risk but remembered the lesson from the earlier experience. Rather than spend the rest of the game wondering about the sacrifice, he played it and won a fine victory.

Less explicable is Tal's explanation of his thoughts about another sacrifice in a later game against Polugayevsky:

> . . . I thought for fifty minutes over a tempting piece sacrifice, each minute becoming more and more convinced that it would not work. And when everything was quite clear, I suddenly became angry with myself for wasting such a lot of time and – sacrificed! Within a few moves, which I had foreseen quite clearly, Polugayevsky repulsed the attack and it was all over.

The conflict here is between intuition and cold logic. A chess player's thoughts are rarely a convergent process, leading inexorably to the move which must be played. Far more often, they involve a process of exploration, which at some stage suggests a move which one wants to play. Then more analysis follows to convince oneself that the intuitively suggested move is indeed the right one. Tal's convincing proof that his intuition was faulty so annoyed him that he had to punish himself by making the move anyway.

Such an error from a great master is hard to understand because Tal knew the move was wrong even before he played it. More common blunders are those which one notices as soon as the piece has left one's hand. Various attempts have been made to classify such mistakes, notably by Ilyin-Zhenevsky in his article 'The Psychology of Chess Mistakes' in *Shakhmatny Listok*, 1928. He produced eight categories of chess mistake, explaining that his task had not been to produce a definitive list, but merely to show that such a classification ought to be possible. His selection of types of blunder, as well as other later refinements and additions, seem all to fall under three broad headings:

1 Loss of concentration

This can strike at any time, but there are three particularly common cases. Firstly, it is all too easy to make the 'natural' move without thinking. Either an 'obvious' reply to a threat, or a move to which the opponent has an 'obvious' answer can be played without checking for the existence of alternatives to these apparently forced moves. That is simply failing to submit one's choice of move to the normal rigorous checking procedures. It is the syndrome best expressed as 'I can play this one without thinking'. The two other most common causes of loss of concentration both occur after the game has passed a crisis. Either when one has reached a position of clear advantage after complications, or when one has just emerged intact from a period of difficult defence, these are the moments when blunders caused by relaxation are most common.

2 The desire to follow forced variations

Most typical of this type of blunder is the blunder in pursuit of brilliancy. A player sees one beautiful variation which wins for him and becomes so infatuated with it that he fails to examine the position thoroughly in the search for alternatives for his opponent. A quiet move in the middle of an apparently forced variation is all too easily overlooked. The desire to pursue the analysis leads to a concentration on forcing continuations, simply in order to be able to proceed further. The main road is so brightly lit that one becomes blind to side turnings. This can just as easily be a cause for the blunder of omission. A move which is so strong that it leaves an opponent with no adequate reply can surprisingly easily be discarded because one can find no move for the opponent, and therefore cannot continue the analysis, which therefore shifts its attention in other directions. There is a side-effect of this same problem, which is the confusion easily arising when the forced variations of one's calculations lead to no clear results. Especially in positions where there are two possible plans, neither of which leads clearly to forced gains, it is easy to go wrong by trying to keep all options open for too long. Even if the forced variation does not work, it seems too tempting to try to keep it in reserve in case it is useful later! Confusion is caused by the non-existence of a concrete answer to the questions of the position.

3   Errors of perception

Perhaps the most common errors of all, when one just overlooks something quite obvious, 'forgets' where a piece is, or completely misses the legality of a crucial move. There is a curious connection here with the manner in which a chess player focuses his attention on the board. Most players will appear to be concentrating intensely on the position in front of them. In general, however, their thoughts will be some moves distant from what they are looking at. Hardly surprising, therefore, that errors of perception occur, perhaps caused by interference between the position seen and that reached in calculation. Some strong players have the habit of occasionally continuing their thoughts staring not at the board, but at the ceiling. This might have the effect of removing the potentially harmful board position from one's gaze, but more often it seems calculated simply to give the eyes a rest.

As Ilyin-Zhenevsky pointed out, there is a common theme running through all these blunder types: the board changes, but ideas stay the same. Even the perceptual errors are most commonly caused by the disappearance in a calculated variation of a previously solid feature of the position. The chess player's mind refuses to accept the alteration and an error results.

Perhaps the main lesson for the chess player is that flexibility of mind and emotion can be a master's greatest asset. To be able to assess each position objectively, without regard to its previous history and to be able to cope with changes in fortune during a single game – these are the principle emotional problems which a chess player must overcome if he is not to add to the enormous literature of chess blunders.

Let us conclude this chapter with four examples of the blunders of world champions which illustrate some of the points mentioned above.

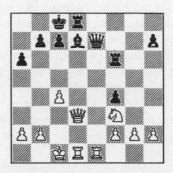

In the first diagram, taken from the game Keres-Alekhine, Margate 1937, Alekhine's queen is attacked by the white rook. The abrupt finish was 1 ... ♛b4? 2 ♛xd7+ and Black had to resign since 2 ... ♖xd7 3 ♖e8+ forces mate in one more move. This seems to be a purely optical blunder; the move 3 ♖e8 is easily missed in the position of the diagram because firstly the black queen is blocking the route to the fatal square, but also that square is at present under the control of both rook and bishop. That all three obstacles can be removed within a couple of moves is a possibility easily overlooked, though one would not expect such a shallow blunder from a world champion very often.

The second position is just as simple an oversight by the man who interrupted Alekhine's reign as world champion. The position is from the game Lasker-Euwe, Nottingham 1936. Black's more harmonious pieces and pawns give him every hope for an endgame victory. His knight is attacked by the white king. Instead of moving the knight or defending it, Euwe blundered with the decision to counterattack the white knight. The sequel was 1 ... ♗a5? 2 b4! ♗xb4 3 ♘c2 and Black, with two pieces now under attack, must lose knight or bishop and with it the game. Euwe's mistake here comes under the category of exaggerated belief in forced variations. White's knight is attacked and therefore it must move. Wrong – he had 'forgotten' the intermezzo 2 b4, luring the bishop onto a vulnerable square.

The next example is another of Euwe's blunders. Playing Black in this position against Flohr in their 1937 match, he has been conducting a powerful attack and now has several roads to victory, of which the most simple is 1 ... ♖xb2, leaving Black a piece ahead and winning comfortably. Instead, he chose the tempting 1 ... ♖g3 pinning the white queen to her king. He must surely have expected instant resignation, but was instead startled by the reply 2 ♔c2! stepping out of the pins on both rank and file. Now 2 ... ♖xf3 is met by 3 de. Overlooking this simple king retreat can only be explained by loss of concentration caused by relaxation on reaching a winning position. One might also ascribe a small responsibility to the optical element; the square c2 is not available to the white king in the position under consideration, but only becomes possible after the rook has moved. Nevertheless, had Euwe even considered the possibility that White might have a defence, he would surely have found the king move.

Finally we revert to Alekhine for a more complicated example of a double blunder. This position occurred shortly before the end of the game Eliskases-Alekhine, Hastings 1936-7. The correct result should be a draw after 1 ... ♗xd2 2 ♕e7+ ♔h6 and White takes perpetual check with the queen on h4 and e7. The actual finish was 1 ... ♘df3+ 2 ♔g2 ♘xd2? 3 ♕e7+ ♔h8 4 ♕e8+ ♔g7 agreed draw! Instead, White can win with 5 ♕g8+ ♔f6 6 ♗e6! and the threat of ♘d5+ will win the queen or mate (6 ... ♕c6+ 7 ♘d5+ ♔g5 8 ♕d8+ ♔h5 9 ♕h4 mate, or 6 ... ♕a5 7 ♘d5+ ♔g5 8 h4+ ♔h5 9 ♘f6 mate). The details of this analysis are not at all important, except to mention that Eliskases would surely have seen it had he even considered the possibility of 6 ♗e6. But that move of the bishop is not at all a forcing move, so the temptation is not to analyse it. Perhaps more important, he had certainly seen that he had no more than a draw after 1 ... ♗xd2, so was disinclined to shift his sights above the level of half a point. It was not so much a question of not seeing 6 ♗e6 , he did not even look for it. Alekhine's blunder in allowing the combination is perhaps less excusable since, with his king under fire from so many white pieces, he must be aware of the danger. As so often in the case of a double oversight, one player miscalculates and his opponent then takes his word for it. The chess player might well be advised never to trust his opponent, but we should be loath to offer such advice for fear of possibly detrimental transference effects in real life.

8 Irrationality

We have discussed the role of subjective considerations in influencing a player's decisions, yet this subjectivity only has room to manoeuvre because chess positions do not in general permit a purely objective solution. The opportunities for a player to indulge his stylistic, subjective preferences are many but their boundaries are defined by rational criteria. A chess player selecting a move is like a gourmet choosing the wine to accompany his meal: the food may narrow down his options while still leaving several acceptable alternatives; the rest is a matter of taste.

In this chapter we deal with some aspects of behaviour at the chessboard which go beyond the exercise of subjectivity into the realms of irrationality. Though objectivity cannot rule the totality of a player's thoughts, an objective attitude has long been held to be a *sine qua non* of chess thought. But as we shall see, factors far removed from both the chessboard and 'real life' can also influence a player's moves and his performances. Communication between the two opponents in a game in purely chess terms only takes place through the medium of the pieces on the board, yet their proximity to one another introduces another element to the confrontation which is too easily ignored in any discussion of the game. Consciously or subconsciously all chess players communicate their fears and hopes about the position to their opponents. Confidence may be affected as much by an opponent's behaviour at the chessboard as by the behaviour of his pieces on it. In chess as in other sports there is room for gamesmanship, though it must in fairness be admitted that this mostly occurs below the conscious and intentional level.

As a harmless example, we might mention Hugh Alexander's observations during his game with Alekhine at Margate 1938. He had noticed a nervous mannerism practised by Alekhine, twisting a curl of hair on his forehead when he was worried about his position. Alexander held a clear advantage in the game and Alekhine was anxiously hair-twiddling. In the endgame, Alexander committed an inaccuracy which let his opponent escape. As soon as the move was made, Alekhine released his lock of hair, swept it back and never betrayed further signs of worry as he steered the game back to the safety of a draw. At that moment, said Alexander, he knew that he was not going to win the game, though it was only some moves later when the position on the board made it clear why he was not going to win.

We may assume from this tale that Alekhine was unaware of his own mannerism, else he would not have divulged so openly his feelings about the position. Several contemporary grandmasters have 'complained' about the ability of Karpov to hide his feelings at the board. In bad and even lost positions he remains outwardly calm and composed, which has the effect of introducing some doubt into the opponent's belief that the game is won. The confidence brought by a good position feeds on evidence that the opponent is suffering. If he can hide his misery, the task of winning the game can be emotionally more difficult.

Such behaviour, or more accurately lack of behaviour, can hardly be termed gamesmanship. One might argue that ideally chess should be played in conditions under which the players cannot see one another. Perhaps correspondence chess players would indeed argue that their game is purer because the emotional struggle, caused by proximity, is absent. But even in correspondence chess a friendly message from your opponent, that he thinks his game is in fine shape, when you think it is on the point of collapse, can be singularly disconcerting.

A stronger case for the existence of gamesmanship in chess is provided by instances where behaviour is deliberately altered in order to induce a state of mind in the opponent which causes him to lose his own objectivity. Take this piece of advice on endgame play offered by Belavenets and quoted by Kotov in *Think Like a Grandmaster* (1971):

> The basic rule of endgames is not to hurry. If you have a chance to advance a pawn one square or two, then first of all advance only one square, have a good look round, and only then play forward one more square. Repeating moves in an ending can be very useful. Apart from the obvious gain of time on the clock one notices that the side with the

advantage gains psychological benefit. The defender who has the inferior position cannot stand the strain and makes new concessions, so easing his opponent's task.

In other words, the attacker stands to gain by spinning out his opponent's agony.

Botvinnik, among the reminiscences in his *Selected Games: 1947-70*, recounts an example of a further refinement of the Belavenets technique. He and Paul Keres were helping analyse Geller's adjourned game against Olafsson at Wijk aan Zee 1969. Botvinnik produced an idea which involved bringing back Geller's king from the queenside to e1, then offering the sacrifice of the exchange. Analysis showed that the sacrifice would win whether accepted or declined. The only defect was that it could be prevented.

I nevertheless persuaded Geller that this plan would be successful: firstly his opponent would not suspect it, and would not think to prevent it in time, but would merely observe passively the wanderings of the hostile king. Also since the white king was retracing its steps, Olafsson would be hoping for the position to be repeated three times and he would not want to change the situation himself. 'And finally, Yefim Petrovich', I said, 'rock about on your chair several times, as many players do in a vain attempt to find a plan'.

Keres and Botvinnik arrived soon after the start of the adjournment session and found Geller already in a winning position. They asked what had happened. 'I rocked about', replied Geller, smiling.

In that case Geller's trick was one of dissimulation. He successfully disguised the fact that he knew what he was doing. More commonly, and more crudely, we are all used to players (especially young ones) making their moves with great confidence in order to disguise the fact that they do not know what they are doing.

Psychological gamesmanship in chess first caught the public imagination at the time of the great Fischer-Spassky match in Reykjavik in 1972. Bobby Fischer was frequently, though unjustly, accused of deliberate tactics to disturb his opponent. There is no doubt that Fischer's long spun-out negotiations and disputes with the match organisers did have the effect of disturbing Spassky's play. Facing a man who turned up days late for the start of the match, then defaulted the second game, was no easy task. Yet Fischer's disputes throughout were only with the organisers, his complaints only about the conditions of play. At the board his behaviour was impeccable and his apologies to Spassky rang sincere. Contrary to popular notions, Spassky seemed to reciprocate these friendly feelings. In a press interview after the match he declared: 'Fischer is a man of art, but he is a rare human being in the everyday life of this century. I like Fischer and I think I understand him'.

In the matter of correct behaviour at the board, Fischer seemed to learn an important lesson from one of his games with Tal in the 1959 Candidates tournament. Fischer as White has sacrificed a piece to reach the position shown. Tal (1976) describes the 'psychological duel' which now took place.

> Fischer first wrote down the move 22 Ⅱa1-e1, without doubt the strongest, and wrote it not in his usual English notation but in European, almost Russian! And not very deftly he pushed the scoresheet towards me. 'He's asking me for an endorsement', I thought to myself, but how was I to react? To frown was impossible, if I smiled he would suspect trickery, and so I did the natural thing. I got up and began to walk calmly up and down the stage. I met Petrosian, made some joke with him and he replied. But the 15-year old Fischer . . . sat with a confused expression on his face . . .

Fischer eventually changed his mind and played 22 ♕c6+ allowing Tal to escape and finally win the game with his extra piece. When, after the game, Tal asked why he had not played 22 Ⅱae1, Fischer replied: 'Well, you laughed when I wrote it down!'.

Before that game Fischer had not been in the habit of writing his moves down before playing them. That practice is recommended by the Soviet chess school as a means of breaking one's own concentration momentarily in order to return to the move with an open and naive mind simply to check for the possibility that it might be a crude error. Later in his career Fischer was to decry the practice as an unfair attempt to elicit some reaction from the opponent. The Tal episode had evidently taught him not only that it was unreliable, but even unfair.

Before leaving this topic, we should remark on how few players manage to perform the task of writing moves before playing them in the manner in which it has been prescribed. The recipe indicates the correct procedure to be calculation followed by decision, then inscription, momentary inspection of the board, and finally playing the move. Yet in practice the delay between writing and playing the move is frequently considerable, even outlasting the original thinking process. Several grandmasters frequently embellish their scoresheets with numerous crossings out, indicating changes of mind, even several times on the same move. These alterations are rarely because the move written first was discovered to be incorrect. Indeed, the final decision is sometimes simply a reversion to the move written first, after two or three changes of mind en route. Perhaps this is simply further evidence that the decision-making process consists of two stages: firstly, calculation and judgment lead to a decision of what move one wants to play, then further time is spent gathering supporting evidence for the correctness of the decision – talking oneself into it.

Of course, writing down moves before playing them is just one part of the ritual of behaviour at the board. Each chess master has his own individual patterns of behaviour which regulate his physical and mental attitudes while he is playing. Some will remain seated at the board throughout the session. Others will spend time at the board only when it is their own move, rising urgently from the chair immediately after making a move to pace nervously about the tournament room. Anatoly Karpov seems to like to remain at the board calculating further after playing his move, until he is satisfied with the position, perhaps content that he knows also what his next move will be. Then he rises and looks at the other games in the hall. Effective utilisation of the opponent's clock time in this manner is difficult for most players, who prefer a rest between moves. It is hard to reach concrete decisions without the urgency imposed by the ticking of one's own clock. Perhaps that is why many blunders are made by players whose opponents are short of time. Deprived of their usual rest between moves, and thrown off their balanced routine of a break between moves, they lose their rhythm of thought.

Some routines at the chessboard can only be described as superstitious behaviour. One English grandmaster always removes his wristwatch at the start of a game, using it thereafter to cover the moves on his scoresheet. This behaviour must have been assumed by others to have a mystical significance, for several lesser British players have copied the habit. In all cases, however, it has failed to lift their play to grandmaster level. Another leading player is superstitious about the pen he uses, while clothes also feature prominently among superstitious fetishes. Several young players show a marked reluctance to change their shirts while they are on a winning streak, but experience generally teaches them that hygienic necessity takes precedence over superstition.

Another common ritual is the solemn adjustment of all the pieces before the game begins, whether they need straightening or not, while one grandmaster goes a stage further in the complex ritualisation process by waiting for his opponent's first move and then, with his own clock running, unhurriedly adjusting all the pieces before replying. All quite harmless, of course, but curious sidelights on the stage of such a rational game. One could argue, of course, that all such superstitions are perfectly logical. Why should one alter behaviour patterns which have previously brought success? Let us give the last word on superstition to Mikhail Tal (1976), who had thoroughly bad luck throughout his return match with Botvinnik in 1961:

> ... by the eighth game ... I finally succeeded in selecting a lucky pencil. Alas, after winning, I left it on the table ... I did not manage to find an adequate replacement.

We cannot leave the subject of irrationality without touching on parapsychology. Is it possible for one player, or a spectator, to influence the mental processes of another player from a distance? The history of important chess matches shows conclusively that, where there is sufficient ill-will across the board, such accusations are bound to be flung about. Even the logical Dr Tarrasch suggested that Emanuel Lasker was using 'witchcraft, hypnotism or such' in order to induce his opponent to make mistakes. On a more mundane level Lasker was also accused by Maroczy of smoking execrable cigars in a deliberate attempt to cause his opponents' play to deteriorate. We should also mention Pal Benko's desperate decision to don a pair of dark glasses to protect him from Tal's hypnotic glare during the 1959

Candidates tournament. That action was reduced to its rightful status as comedy when Tal appeared for their next encounter ready with a huge pair of sunglasses which he solemnly put on as a countergambit.

As we have said, the pure chess confrontation between two players is carried out by proxy through the chess pieces. Many players consider any eye contact to be out of place, perhaps putting the battle on too personal a level. Others seem to have developed an intimidating glare and several grandmasters, including Tal as the most famous example, have acquired a reputation for sudden fierce glances at their opponents. Two chess masters at least have developed their own antidotes to the feared glare: one would respond to the grandmasterly stare by looking fixedly at his opponent's nose, the other preferred to gaze intently just above his head. Staring back and winking has also been tried, but the giggling which tends to result is unseemly in international chess tournaments.

All such stare-related behaviour can hardly be considered a serious attempt to hypnotise an opponent but is merely part of the bigger game of establishing a psychological supremacy over an opponent. Only during the world championship cycle of 1977 and 1978 did serious attention begin to be taken of accusations of hypnotism across the chessboard. Viktor Korchnoi's matches with Boris Spassky and Anatoly Karpov brought accusations and counter-accusations which gave the world of chess an air of mysticism mixed with paranoia which caught the imagination of the press to a degree that chess had rarely, if ever, managed before.

Matters began to get out of hand during the final Candidates match between Boris Spassky and Viktor Korchnoi in Belgrade at the end of 1977. Spassky complained of unidentified forces affecting his concentration. Whether these 'forces' emanated from Korchnoi or from the audience was not made clear, though Spassky appeared to favour the latter explanation. He had a cubicle specially constructed on stage to shield him from the spectators. In this cubicle, he would sit in splendid isolation thinking about his moves as he looked at the position on demonstration boards. He would return to the board only momentarily to execute his moves. In this manner he declared that he was able to overcome the feeling of mental paralysis which overcame him when he sat at the board with Korchnoi. This was not the first time in his career that Spassky had found cause to complain of unidentified forces. A curiously similar incident occurred in the Fischer-Spassky match of 1972, when a request by Spassky led to Fischer's swivel chair being dismantled in a search for electronic devices. Following the acquittal of the chair, suspicion fell on the light fitting above the board. After intense investigations nothing was revealed except for two dead flies.

Spassky's suspicions never reached the level of precise accusations, though at one particularly acrimonious moment in the match with Korchnoi each player seemed convinced that the other was trying to hypnotise him. Korchnoi reports strangely bad moves entering his head at precisely the moment when Spassky began staring at him from his cubicle. But we had to wait for the World Championship match in Baguio City in 1978 for events to take a more serious course and for the first parapsychological chess villain in chess to emerge.

The key figure was Dr Vladimir Zukhar, a psychologist and neurologist attached to the Soviet camp, whose precise function as helper to Karpov was never made clear during the match. Korchnoi had no doubt that the mysterious doctor was waging a parapsychological war from his position towards the front of the auditorium to ruin the challenger's chances of winning the match. There were two explanations advanced at different times by Korchnoi to clarify just how Zukhar was achieving his effect. During the match, Korchnoi protested about the position of Dr Zukhar in the playing hall on the grounds that the man was hypnotising him into playing badly. In private, however, and after the match, he asserted that Dr Zukhar had not so much an ill effect on his own play, but appeared to have an ability to improve Karpov's powers of concentration and to inject the world champion with new energy when he was tiring.

All this sounds rather nonsensical, but should be viewed in the light of recent Soviet research into the paranormal. As early as the 1920s V.M.Bekhterev, a respected pupil of Pavlov, presented several papers on 'Mental Suggestion at a Distance' to Soviet scientific conferences. His work was continued by L.L.Vasiliev, whose results formed the basis for a book, *Experiments in Mental Suggestion* (1963). On a level connected directly with chess, we cannot ignore the work of Dr Vladimir Raikov of the Moscow Psychoneurological Clinic. Dr Raikov's researches have been on the subject of releasing talent in the subconscious, particularly in artistic fields. Henry Gris and William Dick (1979) devote a whole chapter to his experimental results, including an account of a student being hypnotised into believing he was Paul Morphy. Grandmaster Tal was present at the session and played six games of chess with the student, three before and three after hypnosis. Tal observed a great change in his opponent's demeanour and play:

> Before, he looked just what he was, a young man very unsure of himself. Now, under hypnosis, he strode about the room and sat down opposite me with all the authority of a champion player! It was a complete transformation. Now he was expansive, brimming with energy and imagination, daring and at times brilliant. He was immeasurably better.

The results of the games were 3-0 to Tal before hypnosis and 2½-½ to Tal after hypnosis. Bearing in mind our knowledge of Tal as a generous man, these can hardly be considered as conclusive evidence that the student's play had really improved, but we can be sure that his confidence and style were certainly altered in the hypnotic state.

Add to this some further evidence of parapsychology in the Soviet Union and we can be sure that the subject is viewed with some awe:

> From CIA agents come reports that the Russians were able to influence telepathically the behaviour of people, alter their emotions or health, and even kill at long distance by using only psychic powers (Gris and Dick, 1979).

Both Spassky and Korchnoi had grown up in a culture abounding with such rumours of parapsychological possibilities. It is not surprising that their fears occasionally rise to the surface.

This is not the place to enter into a long discussion of what might really be possible in the sphere of psycho-kinesis, or hypnosis at a distance. The Cambridge parapsychologist Dr Carl Sargent finds it more plausible that Zukhar was supporting Karpov than that he might have been hypnotising Korchnoi against his will. He suggests the possibility that Zukhar had established a strong rapport with Karpov in pre-match hypnotic sessions, enabling him to use that rapport to support Karpov during the games.

Even this may be fanciful, though one thing is clear: whatever the parapsychological effect a man like Zukhar might be capable of, it can only be a fraction as effective as the psychological effect caused by the mere belief that he is doing something. Once Korchnoi had complained about the mysterious 'hypnotist', Dr Zukhar became a valuable weapon for Karpov. He had only to be in the same room in order to affect adversely Korchnoi's emotional state.

As far as is known, such paranormal forces as were complained of by Spassky and Korchnoi cannot be shielded or hidden from by retreating to a secluded cubicle or by having the offending person moved to the back of the hall. Such psycho-kinetic effects are not diminished by walls or distance. The main evidence against any paranormal explanations of the complaints of these two grandmasters is that their play in both cases improved after taking their home-made remedies. Had there been anything serious to worry about, there would have been no marked improvement. Whether a parapsychological disturbance of players' thought processes is possible at all must remain an open question. These case histories seem to admit more easily of a purely psychological explanation.

9 Therapeutic Value?

Chesse-play is a good and wittie exercise for the mind of some kind of men, and fit for such melancholy persons as are idle and have impertinent thoughts, or troubled with cares, nothing better to distract their minde and alter their meditations; invented (some say) by the General of an army in a famine to keepe his soldiers from mutiny.

But if it proceed from overmuch study, in such a case it may doe more harme than good; it is a game too troublesome for some men's braines, too full of anxiety, all out as bad as study; and besides it is a testy cholericke game and very offensive to him that loseth the mate.

Robert Burton, *Anatomy of Melancholy*, 1626.

The game of Chess is not merely an idle amusement; several very valuable qualities of the mind, useful in the course of human life, are to be acquired and strengthened by it, so as to become habits ready on all occasions: for life is a kind of Chess, in which we have often points to gain, and competitors or adversaries to contend with, and in which there is a vast variety of good and ill events that are, in some degree, the effect of prudence, or of the want of it.

Benjamin Franklin, *The Morals of Chess*, 1786.

Throughout the ages, chess has had its propagandists and its detractors; the former so much in love with the game as to be blind to any possible harmful side-effects, the opponents of chess equally one-sided in their critical attitudes. On the one side of the argument, chess is praised for its beneficial effect on various human faculties. According to Benjamin Franklin, it teaches us foresight, circumspection and caution. Later writers added will-power and self-control to the list, while Wilhelm Steinitz (1889) saw no limits to the power of chess:

It is almost universally recognised as a healthy mental exercise, which in its effects on the intellectual faculties is akin to that of physical gymnastics on the conservation and development of bodily strength. Moreover, the cultivation of the game seems also to exercise a direct influence on the physical condition of chess players and the prolongation of their lives, for most of the celebrated chess masters and authors on the game have reached a very old age, and have preserved their mental powers unimpaired in some instances up to their very last moments.

This was indeed the generally accepted nineteenth-century view of the value of chess; as Adolf Anderssen expressed it, chess was 'the gymnasium of the mind'. Yet as the game developed into an ever more competitive sport, it developed a strong undercurrent of dissenting views. The detractors could also produce evidence to demonstrate the power of chess as a possibly malign influence. Steinitz himself had died in an asylum for the insane, while the history of world championship chess from Morphy to the present day is littered with symptoms of paranoia. The encouragement of chess among schoolchildren has been opposed on the grounds that pursuit of the game develops all the worst features of competitiveness: greedy ambition and a delight in tempting mistakes from rivals. Yet a recent study supported by the Ministry of Education in Venezuela claims results demonstrating that the study of chess in schools leads to an improvement in IQ scores.

The question is simple: Is Chess Good For You? The claims on both sides are extravagant: chess may drive sane men mad, according to one view, yet has proved of undoubted usefulness in therapy for mental disorders. Where does the truth lie? Let us examine some case histories, beginning with the evidence for the prosecution. Many witnesses may be called, but the heavyweights are Morphy, Steinitz and Rubinstein.

The story of Paul Morphy is well known. At the age of twenty-one he crossed the Atlantic to Europe to challenge the strongest masters, having already proved himself without peer in America. His victories demonstrated convincingly that he was the greatest player of his day. On his return to America he tried unsuccessfully to practise in his chosen profession at law. He wanted to be a lawyer but found that he was only taken seriously as a chess player. He became progressively more disturbed and developed delusions of persecution centred around accusations that his brother was trying to steal his patrimony. On Morphy's death from apoplexy, the verdict of the New York *Sun* was that the strain of playing blindfold chess had produced a 'brain fever' which drove him insane and then killed him.

The career of the first official World Champion, Wilhelm Steinitz, lasted considerably longer than that of Morphy, but the end of his life was similarly tragic. Delusions led to his being committed to an asylum where he died at the age of sixty-four. Morphy had played almost no chess during the last thirty years of his life; Steinitz had continued competing in tournaments to within a year of his demise.

Finally, the great Polish grandmaster Akiba Rubinstein provides perhaps the saddest story. Always uncommunicative and nervous, his condition slowly deteriorated into catatonia. His polite shyness was such that he would not sit at the board when it was his opponent's move, while his mental problems included an imaginary fly which bothered him during tournament games and kept him awake at night. Yet during his best years Rubinstein was one of the few grandmasters who could be considered a genuine contender for the world championship. Finally the strain of tournament chess proved too great for his delicate mental state. His last twenty years were spent away from chess competition in poverty. He died at the age of eighty.

One may list many more great chess players who suffered symptoms of mental disorder but the question remains whether the obsessive nature of chess can be held to blame for their condition. Were these men obsessive characters, psychological misfits who found in chess an outlet for their unusual talents and a refuge from the real world?

Before approaching that question, let us examine the evidence from the other side. There are many cases of chess showing its value in the therapy of mental disorders. The following is a typical example, reported by R.Pakenham-Walsh (1949). He writes of a patient at Lancaster Moor Hospital, suffering from recurrent mania. Within the narrow confines of the hospital, he had long been regarded as almost invincible at chess. Ordinary methods of treatment had brought about no improvement in his mental condition, but his strength at chess provided a means of re-introducing him to normal society. He was taken to Lancaster chess club, where he lost a game to their top board player, but impressed sufficiently to be incorporated into their team. His success led to a great interest in chess at the hospital, which formed its own team and played several matches. Dr Pakenham-Walsh reports that the regular players in the team comprised one case of recurrent mania, six schizophrenics, one manic depressive and one high-grade defective. The matches were very popular, 'especially on one occasion when our hosts provided beer instead of tea'. (In that respect at any rate they seem to resemble most normal club chess teams.) For the record, the result of their first match was a 4-4 draw with the City club.

Dr Pakenham-Walsh, even before this episode, appeared to have some belief in the applications of chess as recreational therapy. He thought it an appropriate exercise since 'the intricacies of chess should have a special appeal for those whose minds are absorbed with abstract problems, particularly schizophrenics'. For that reason one might expect a higher incidence of chess interest among mental patients, though he adds that 'the schizophrenic is by nature unsociable, and may prefer to work out imaginary games by himself or solve the problems found in newspapers'. He ends his account with general approval of the role of their chess-playing adventures in improving the condition of his patients and with an intriguing suggestion that chess might be used in similar cases as more than merely a form of recreational therapy. He suggests that it might provide a form of personality and intelligence test which could be used to detect and measure differences in a patient before and after treatment. The cautious player might become reckless, or the attacking player defensive. Others have speculated on the effect of such brain operations as lobotomy and leucotomy on chess skill but as far as we know no such surgery has been performed on strong players. 'I am already convinced', concludes Dr Pakenham-Walsh, 'that an attack of insanity does not necessarily interfere with the competence of a good chess player'.

Others have reported more specifically on the benefits of chess in the therapy of individuals, usually suffering from forms of schizophrenia. The game provides an outlet for hostile impulses and it is seen as a social experience in which the acts and wishes of another person have to be taken into consideration. The rules of the game provide a discipline which has to be adhered to and the emotions generated by the game have been used to touch off valuable digressions in which patients are able to talk about their feelings. Above all, the fact that chess is a game and not real has made it easier for patients to exert some control over their emotions and to master them, at least to some extent.

So properly controlled, the game of chess can provide a small world through which the mentally disturbed can be encouraged to come to terms with the real, larger world. The chessboard may provide a means of expression and communication for someone who is unable to utilise more normal means. Players of chess are exchanging ideas, carrying on a discussion or even argument within highly structured rules and in an environment in which everything is under the control of the player. For anyone unable to cope with the unpredictability of the real world, chess has much to recommend it. But what of those who initially can cope with reality but nevertheless choose to devote themselves to chess?

At face value, the assets of chess seem clear, though at different levels of play the lessons taught by chess may not be the same. Benjamin Franklin ends his account of the benefits of chess with the following:

> And lastly, we learn by Chess the habit of not being discouraged by present bad appearances in the state of our affairs; the habit of hoping for a favourable chance, and that of persevering in the search of resources. The game is so full of events, there is such a variety of turns in it, the fortune of it is so sudden to vicissitudes, and one so frequently, after contemplation, discovers the means of extricating oneself from a supposed insurmountable difficulty, that one is encouraged to continue the contest to the last, in hopes of victory from our skill; or, at least, from the negligence of our adversary.

Sadly, Benjamin Franklin betrays in that paragraph his lack of skill as a chess player. Any stronger player will have learnt precisely the opposite lesson from chess: that a lost position is made no better by a Micawberish hope that something will turn up. One must fight and preserve as much optimism as possible when affairs are bad; one learns the art of opportunism, but one also learns not to rely on the mistakes of the adversary. Above all, chess teaches us to live with the consequences of our own decisions, whether they were good or bad.

Of Franklin's other beneficial lessons of chess: foresight, circumspection and caution, there can be no disagreement. But before rushing into a wholehearted recommendation of chess, we ought to compare its value with that of other games. Might one not, for example, make the same claims as have been advanced for chess in favour of Space Invaders? There is a pastime which clearly teaches us foresight, circumspection and caution. Also one might add concentration, realism and manual dexterity. Yet nobody (as far as we know) has advocated Space Invaders as deserving time on a school curriculum. Any such suggestion, of course, is facetious, but gives the lie to the facile explanation why chess is good for us. We must look deeper into the nature of chess to understand its effects and discover whether the faculties developed through the game of chess may be transferable to other activities. To argue that a game which demands concentration and self-control necessarily teaches us to apply those qualities in other areas is as mistaken in the case of chess as it is for Space Invaders.

The disciplined thought which chess requires is unlike that of most other games. Concentration is essential, of course, but more than the unflagging attention necessary to carry out an endless routine or repetitive task. In chess, unlike most video games, each game leads to a totally new position, in which one may be applying techniques already learned, but the conclusions and decisions will necessarily be novel. This constant stimulus of new problems, or at least variations on old problems, is what gives chess a life of its own. Unlike games with cards or dice, chance, in theory anyway, plays no part. And finally, chess is a game of complete information – all the pieces are fully visible and their powers calculable. In practical terms, chess provides an infinitely variable world, but one in which at any given moment everything is known. It is an ideal model for anyone who wants complete control over his own destiny.

Just as the mini-world of the chessboard can be a stepping-stone towards learning to control one's life in the real world, so can it be a step in the opposite direction. Obsession with chess, as with anything else, can cause alienation from the real world. Stefan Zweig's *Schachnovelle*, 'The Royal Game', gives a brilliant account of the chess obsession taking over a healthy mind. But that is a tale primarily of obsession, not of chess. To an obsessive personality, a preoccupation with chess may indeed be considered dangerous, but taken in moderation it can be as beneficial as any other drug. Let the last word go to grandmaster Mieses (1940):

> I consider it very questionable indeed that chess talent implies any gift, even in minor proportions, for other fields of mental activity; or that aptitude for chess enriches the mind universally. In this connection I should like to warn young people, at all events those yet at their studies, against any too intensive preoccupation with the game. It is true that

chess is one of the noblest of the mental recreations, a real 'stamping ground' of cleverness; but it contains a world all of its own, an abstract world of strange charm. Whoever has once experienced this fascination may easily succumb to it and thereby develop one-sidedly; particularly since chess, as fundamentally a game of combat, lends powerful impetus to one's ambition to improve in it. It is precisely the talented youngster who is most exposed to this danger. Only he who has attained a certain degree of completion to his general education and spiritual development and whose character has passed the moulding stage may devote himself freely to the goddess of chess without fear of the consequences. The noble game has its depths, in which many a fine and gentle soul, alas, has vanished.

Should a future government of any country decide that chess has a potentially harmful effect on its practitioners, they could well consider adopting this paragraph of Mieses as the mandatory health warning on every chess set.

10 The Origins of Skill

In previous chapters we have considered chess as a highly intensive form of pattern recognition, and given an account of the sinister urges which, according to some psychoanalysts, provide its motive force.

We now turn to a less recondite matter – the social factors which seem to be related to aptitude and enthusiasm. What kind of person is likely to be attracted by chess, and what cultural background is likely to foster an interest in it? In favour of chess, it has often been remarked that today it is classless, and transcends differences of race and nationality. This is true and is certainly a powerful asset. On the other hand there are marked differences in the skill of different groups. Certain nations do perform consistently better than others. Some countries possess more enduring chess traditions than others, and it has been claimed that such traditions are closely related to a general cultural or educational level of the population. Indeed, some would want to say that chess prowess is an index of culture.

Soviet policy, of course, represents the most obvious self-conscious awareness of the importance of chess in the community. When Cuba fell within the Soviet orbit, and Castro rose to power, a trade delegation headed by Mikoyan included Grandmaster Keres in its entourage. But before the intense politicising of chess, which had its roots in the 1917 revolution ('Chess cannot be apolitical as in capitalist countries' – Ilyin-Zhenevsky), there had been no attempt on the part of governments to use chess as a weapon for raising the cultural level of the broad masses. Hence, without State intervention, any relation which can be observed between power and chess is a by-product rather than a direct consequence of social policy. We might start by supposing that the more powerful, or the more prosperous, a nation, the greater its skill at chess. This is a well-known argument, and in the history of chess it is roughly true. But it is probably not distinctive. An interest in other arts (or sciences) may also be correlated with economic power. In Marxist terminology, such cultural achievements would all be part of a 'superstructure' controlled by an economic base. But perhaps this argument should be modified because totalitarian powers have been known to exert a control over the content of art and the methods of scientific research. Chess could be assumed to be a more accurate reflection of power and prestige because its abstract nature renders it immune to criticism.

Let us take a brief and over-simplified view of the history of chess. The oldest European authors flourished in Spain and Portugal around 1500, chess having already been introduced by the Arabs in the late Middle Ages. During the Renaissance the names of Polerio and Greco stand out in Italy. In the eighteenth century, when France dominated the whole of Europe, chess was seen at its best in the play of Philidor and Labourdonnais. Finally, in the nineteenth and twentieth centuries, the focus of strength shifted towards Great Britain, Germany and the United States, quite apart from what might be called its cultivated explosion in the USSR.

It is of considerable interest to note that the great chess writer Réti seemed unaware of this explosion. But then, in 1923, its effects had hardly begun to be felt, especially in Central Europe. (Indeed, the real mastery of the Soviets only became apparent after the end of the 1939-45 War when it was manifested in the great Groningen Tournament of 1946, won by Botvinnik; in the World Championship Tournament in 1948, again won by Botvinnik; and in the Radio Matches of 1945 in which both the Americans and British were convincingly trounced by large margins.)

What concerned Réti was the supposed American threat to European ideals, and in expressing this concern he was the first author to claim the detection of cultural traits in the style of individuals:

> Today we see in chess the fight of aspiring Americanism against the old European intellectual life: a struggle between the technique of Capablanca, a *virtuoso* in whose play one can find nothing tangible to object to, and between great European masters, all of them artists, who have the qualities as well as the faults of artists in the treatment of the subject they devote their lives to: they experimentalise and in striving

after what is deep down, they overlook what is near to hand.

At the last London Congress, with the time limit so unfavourable to the European type, they succumbed before Capablanca. Yet they go on investigating and building further. Who will come out of this struggle victorious? Nobody can prophesy the answer. But one thing is certain. If Americanism is victorious in chess, it will also be so in life. For in the idea of chess and the development of the chess mind we have a picture of the intellectual struggle of mankind. (Réti, 1923)

At the least this is well written, but, as so often with fine rhetoric, the spell of the words detracts from the force of the argument. Is it really true that Capablanca's limpid style is lacking in soul, a matter of effortless technique, and in some (unclear) way symptomatic of 'Americanism'? One might just as well say that Botvinnik's resilient style is typical of ths class struggle within International Communism. But once started on the game of detecting national characteristics, Réti gets lured into making one further step. He adds a footnote to his peroration: 'I should like to add here, that the Americanism of Capablanca's play shows itself in a milder, more attractive garb, probably (as was the case with Morphy) by reason of his Latin ancestry'. Elsewhere in the book, Réti finds reflected in the 'broad design' of Schlechter's play the 'airiness of Viennese art and music'. A great deal of this is a harmless 'poetism' – a conjuring up of analogies which may help one to appreciate the style of a particular master. But such observations clearly have no scientific validity: they would only have this if the games played by masters in country x could be stylistically distinguished (without knowing their origin) from those played by masters in country y. This seems unlikely. What is interesting about Réti's poetic suggestions is the ease with which certain characteristics can be projected on to an abstract system. Chess becomes an ink-blot (projection) test, and the psychologist might feel inclined to say that in the passages quoted we learn more about Réti than about chess. More serious, however, interpretations of this kind provide an unfortunate precedent for the frenzied attacks of Alekhine on 'Jewish chess'. This we shall consider shortly.

For the moment let us abandon the dreams of racial origin reflected in chess, and turn to the indisputable evidence that some countries consistently perform better than others. Roughly, as Réti divined, excellence in chess mirrors the wealth of the nation. This has certainly been true in the past, and even today the Third World has produced very few great players. Perhaps this is not surprising, but this picture of the growth of chess spontaneously following the increased leisure made possible by wealth is complicated, as we have already noticed, by the extensive state support made possible in Communist countries. The dominance of the Soviets since the 1939-45 War has been manifested in the Olympiads with an almost monotonous regularity. It is, however, the curious exceptions and irregularities which are of more interest. Lying behind the performance of the Soviet team we generally find Hungary, Yugoslavia and the USA. But Poland, which it might be thought has contributed a substantial amount to cultural achievements, lies a good way behind in the race, in spite of its great chess tradition – one thinks of Akiba Rubinstein (1881-1961). Similarly, the sudden flowering of chess talent in the United Kingdom, with its crop of grandmasters in the 1970s, would hardly be attributed to economic prosperity. It has been said that high unemployment is a useful precondition for producing good chess players in culturally developed countries. One might compare the UK in the 1980s with the USSR in the 1950s. Although the USSR has never had unemployment there are few satisfying outlets for creative work, and the opportunities afforded by a career in chess must have seemed attractive.

In any case, the competitive aspect of the olympiads can be overstressed. Just as important seems to be the friendly rivalry between players from very different backgrounds. A similar spirit, incidentally, is strongly expressed in international correspondence chess – in spite of the fact that the players do not actually meet they sometimes express a wish to help each other if they do visit each other's countries. Such friendly relations transcend the competitive spirit of winning (or losing) which brings glory and gold medals to victorious teams. Not for nothing is the FIDE motto: 'Gens Una Sumus'.

The establishment of a 'league table' of nations is somewhat ephemeral, but if we were pressed to define the social conditions which make for success, we would cite (a) the existence of an autonomous strong chess tradition, and (b) substantial financial support for training and education. This will tend to produce masters and grandmasters which, in turn, will set a standard for the rest. It is indeed gratifying that private enterprise in the United Kingdom has in recent years given such support to the organization of chess events.

It is, however, worth taking a closer look at one particular cultural group because it claims a disproportionate number of grandmasters and because its success is not easily attributed to extrinsic social factors. Alexander (1973) has pointed out that people always ask: 'Why are the Russians so good at chess?', but almost never the equally pertinent question, 'Why are Jews so good at chess?'. As we have hinted, the question about Jewish prowess is more interesting and baffling because no organizational support for this group is evident. Hence, Alexander suggests that a specific interest in chess may have arisen in Jews because of a need to excel in activities other than those from which they have been so long excluded. Indeed, Alexander buttresses his argument by pointing out that, once support had been provided by Israel, then the fighting qualities needed for top-level chess declined. In 1973 there were no Israeli grandmasters. This is an ingenious hypothesis. Apart from the need to excel, one could add the proverbial Jewish enjoyment of argument, and the precision which goes with good argument, as contributory factors to success. It is perhaps significant in this connection that Akiba Rubinstein is said to have abandoned the study of the Talmud in order to devote his life to chess.

Whatever the explanation of Jewish success the facts are beyond dispute. Indeed, Alexander (perhaps tongue in cheek) claimed that the chess world, at least in former times, could be ordered into four groups from strong to weak:

> Russian Jews
> Russian Non-Jews
> Non-Russian Jews
> Non-Russian Non-Jews

The implication is that the last group has not got much going for them, and had better pack their bags and leave the tournament hall.

It is a plausible enterprise to consider the potential which cultural, or racial, groups seem to possess for chess excellence, and to speculate about the reasons, but considerable caution is needed because of the controversial assessment of the roles of genetic and environmental contributions in any area of intellectual achievement. As we argued previously, it is even more difficult to make out a serious case for the existence of racial (or cultural) characteristics in the way in which a person plays chess. It will be remembered that Réti saw an Americanism in Capabalanca's play expressed in a 'milder and more attractive garb by reason of his Latin ancestry'. This observation should probably not be taken too seriously – perhaps it is no more really than saying of a style of argument that it is 'very French'. But a shocking (and slightly dotty) echo of it was heard in Nazi-occupied Holland in 1941. Under the title 'Jewish and Aryan Chess', an article under Dr Alekhine's name appeared in *Deutsche Zeitung in lem Nederland*, and was reprinted in *Deutsche Schachzeitung*. After the War a bitter argument raged about the authorship, but (according to Golombek, 1977) many years later, after Alekhine's third wife had died in Paris, among his papers the manuscript of the disputed articles was discovered in his handwriting. Lacking in sustained argument, and full of abuse, the original article tried to maintain that Jewish chess is essentially defensive, materialistic, and opportunistic. Three quotes are sufficient to bring out the impoverished quality of his thought.

> It is becoming more and more apparent that the purely negative Jewish conception of chess (Steinitz – Lasker – Rubinstein – Nimzowitsch) perverted, for half a century, the logical development of our art of battle . . .
> Staunton's defeat at the hands of Anderssen was in reality much, much more than a decision between two chess masters; its significance lay in the fact that it spelt the defeat of the English-Jewish idea of defence at the hands of the Germano-European idea of aggression . . .
> Are the Jews, as a race, gifted for chess? After a chess experience of thirty years, I should answer this question as follows: Yes, the Jews are extremely well endowed with the ability to exploit the ideas of chess and the practical potentialities entailed; but, as yet, no real chess artist of Jewish origin has existed. I would mention (and only give outstanding names) the following creative representatives of Aryan chess . . . As to the 'Jewish harvest' for the same historical period, one cannot but call it poor and meagre. Apart from Steinitz and Lasker, various groups might profitably be examined in historical sequence . . .

Three articles of this kind appeared under Alekhine's name, the last one published in *Pariser Zeitung*. They were translated and reprinted in *Chess* (August 1941, October 1941, January 1942). It is difficult to believe how anyone could have taken them seriously. Their sole interest, apart from their blatant distortion of truth, is the way in which a purely intellectual exercise can be used as a vehicle for political propaganda. Any rational consideration shows that it is dubious (on psychological grounds) to read defensiveness, or opportunism, or anything else, into the styles of particular racial groups. People will find there what they want to find, and overlook what they want to overlook.

What other groups can be characterized by a special interest, or lack of interest, in chess? What about women? It is indeed true that these days a spectator at any major tournament will see in the audience a large variety of different types of individuals, of all ages, classes and professions (especially, it might be noted, a collection of eager young schoolboys), but the singular fact stands out that they will be predominantly male. We might conclude that women are less interested in chess than men, and hence that they are not so good at it. But are they less good because of a lack of interest, or less interested because they do not do so well? There are a variety of problems here, and our personal experience suggests that we should tread with care. Of course, the possibly stereotyped assumption springs to mind – women (as a whole) tend to be more practical than men, and less interested in abstract thought. That fits the facts with which we are concerned, but it is the source of the sex difference, rather than the manifestation of it, which is of interest here.

Under the sub-title 'From a Woman', Leonore Gallet wrote a letter about chess to Edward Lasker, which appears along with other interesting letters, in *Chess for Fun and Chess for Blood* (Lasker, 1942).

> . . . I don't consider it possible for any woman, though, to become a chess master. She won't be able to keep her mind on the game long enough without letting her thoughts wander. When she thinks of a beautiful move she is liable to think how beautiful she looks in making it. Then there is that sale she saw advertised! Oh, and so many other things!
>
> You always say chess trains one to concentrate. I don't believe a word of it!

Even at the time of writing this comment was factually wrong. Vera Menchik, probably the strongest woman player ever, killed by a flying-bomb in 1944, held her own with male masters. But it is the tone of the letter (fitting the male stereotype of femininity) which might perturb the adherents of feminism. It would seem that not all women regard themselves today in the same way as they evidently did forty years ago . How do we set about explaining the inferiority of women in the male-dominated sphere of chess? There are at least three rough theories which could account for the discrepancy between the sexes, but before considering them it is worth pointing out that we have sometimes heard the (true) statement, 'Women *don't* play chess well', instantly paraphrased as the (indeterminate) statement, 'Women *can't* play chess well'.

First, there is the cultural deprivation theory which attributes any lack of achievement by women to the way in which our existing society is organized. In a broad sense the central notion is incontestable – women are still discriminated against in a wide variety of ways. More important in the present context, it is assumed that their mentality is in some way different from that of men – 'intuitive' as opposed to 'logical'. Radical feminists attribute such differences (and any others they can find) to a cultural conditioning which starts with infancy. On top of any specific differences in mentality, there is the undoubted fact, expressed in Leonore Gallet's letter, that women have more claims on their attention than men, a difference which will persist until sex roles are equalised. Consistent with this theory is the fact that, in most Western countries at any rate, girls are not encouraged at a tender age to take an interest in chess, just as they are less motivated to take an interest in the sciences. There are, of course, striking exceptions to this generalization, but statistically it seems to be roughly true. Sex roles, whether male or female, tend to be inculcated by insidious social pressures.

Outside our own culture there are some interesting differences. The USSR, and more specifically the Caucasian Republic of Georgia, have produced at least four 'lady grandmasters' – the famous Nona Gaprindashvili (who won the World Title in 1962), Maya Chiburdanidze (the reigning World Champion), Nana Ioselani, and Nini Gurieli. This flowering of talent in one Soviet Republic is explained by Kotov (1980) as due to the dedication and enthusiasm of V.Karseladze and his chess school. It remains, however, of interest that such players do not generally compete successfully against the best men players, and their grades are not equivalent to their male counterparts. Historically, the case of Vera Menchik, trained by the Hungarian grandmaster Geza Maroczy, has already been mentioned. Some male grandmasters, including Euwe, were her victims, and a club existed of male players who had been beaten by her. How she would have performed in contemporary chess is unclear. On the whole, it seems fair to say that even with intensive training women do not do as well as men.

The second theory is really related to consciousness induced by cultural deprivation. The aspirations, or expectations, about women's performance may exert a limiting force upon their skill. Before Roger Bannister ran a mile in four minutes it seemed an impossible feat, but now several people have done it, and it does not seem extraordinary. (The chess analogy would be Philidor's feat in the eighteenth century of playing two simultaneous blindfold games, which was hailed at the time as one of the greatest achievements of mankind. In 1960 the Hungarian international master, Janos Flesch, played 52 games without sight of the board.) The important thing is that an expectation, or rather a norm, especially one held by women themselves, may hold back their competitive skill. In addition, women are generally trained by men, and it seems quite likely that this may induce some feeling of inferiority. (Even in the Soviet Union we know of no woman trainer.) In a sense, they are indoctrinated into playing bad chess. And then, in contrast to their training by men, they tend to play only against each other. Hence they fail to qualify for the highest events. There is no break through the norm. At the moment there is no woman rated in the top 300 in the world, and it is probably true to say that since Menchik none has reached the top 100. On this theory, however, the performance of women could be changed if their consciousness were to be transformed. The attempts being made in the Republic of Georgia are a brave step in this direction. Let us hope they will succeed.

There are some interesting analogies. In the nineteenth century, or even in the early years of the twentieth century, the cultural and social background of the typical chess player was generally that of the upper middle classes. It was doubtless considered that chess was an appropriate means of expression for gentlemen of leisure, but inappropriate for others. Today we see chess much more widely diffused in the community, to such an extent that it has a good claim for being classless. A limitation due to social stratification has been annulled. Even more remarkable is the lack of British grandmasters until the 1970s. Indeed, it could be argued that the chess being played by leading British players in the 1960s was about as strong as that of today's strongest women players. What has happened here is that in the 1960s the next goal was not in sight. A breakthrough had to be effected, and once it had occurred, several others were able to exploit it. We have already drawn attention to the four-minute-mile phenomenon, and the same sort of thing seems to have occurred in male chess. On this account women play chess less well than men because their own goals (possibly set by men) are not high enough.

The third theory, which can be divided into two components, is biological. The qualities demanded by high-level chess are, on the whole, less compatible with the female nervous system. The differences between men and women in this sphere are innate rather than culturally conditioned. (This hypothesis may not be true, but it is certainly no more 'sexist' than pointing out that most men are taller than most women.) The lower degree of physical strength shown by women may be correlated with a lower capacity for sustained concentration over a five-hour session. This has its parallel in the notorious effect of the ageing process in male players during the fifth hour of play. Perhaps even more important than a relative inability to concentrate over long periods of time is the ability to sustain that aggression which is vital in the will to win. Nobody would suppose that women are less aggressive as a sex, but men might be inclined to suppose that women do not (for whatever reason) enjoy sustaining aggression in a single-minded way. It has been pointed out, not altogether facetiously, that since women are undoubtedly nicer than men they play chess less well. It has also been claimed that since women are generally less encouraged to be competitive, those who do play serious chess tend to be over-competitive and over-motivated, and hence suffer more from irrationality in their play. Of course, a lot of these views may not be free from (male) stereotypes and preconceptions about female mentality. But just look at the terms which might be used to describe playing chess: sustained, abstracted, combative, absorbed in a geometric matrix. They seem to comprise a rare trait, but one which looks more male than female.

The biological theory finds more specific support in some recent research. It has long been known that women are slightly better at verbal intelligence test items than men, and that conversely men are better at the spatial items. More recently, Jensen (1980) has shown that these differences are more pronounced at the top end of the scales. Thus female intellectual excellence shines in linguistic skills, and male in spatial skills. But, as we have already pointed out, chess seems to be the spatial-intellectual task *par excellence*. Therefore, women would not be expected to be so attracted towards it, nor would they become so good at it. Once again, it must be stressed that there are exceptions to this generalization. Apart from Vera Menchik there was a Mrs Baird in the last century who was a noted problemist.

If this theory were true, then of course women would not be expected to catch up with men. (Nor perhaps would they want to.)

So there are three theories which could account for women's inferiority at chess: forms of social organization in which women's abilities are subjugated (cultural deprivation); associated lower goals and aspirations which are a reflection of such social systems; and innate biological differences. It is not feasible to assess the extent to which these theories interact. The common climate of opinion is to stress the dominating influence of cultural factors. This view is plausible because it is certainly evident over a wide range of behaviour, but it does not follow that it is the sole explanation for a specialised activity such as chess.

These arguments demonstrate the difficulty in attempting to explain why particular groups of individuals excel at the expense of others. We might look at some obvious comparisons. One might ask why particular nations, or social groups, excel at (say) musical composition, or poetry, and there is no very convincing answer. On the whole, one can note only correlations, e.g. the flowering of dramatic and lyric poetry in the Elizabethan Age which coincided with the dominance of the country as a world power, or the Irish literary revival in the early years of the present century with its roots in nationalism and the rediscovery of the Gaelic language, etc. In addition to the lack of exactitude in posing historical or sociological questions of this kind, there is something chauvinistic about comparing groups in this way, something incompatible with the chess ideal, 'We are one people'.

Still, when we are talking about the origins of skill, we must consider the needs of education in chess. For instance, it would be beneficial if there were some kind of test which predicts chess ability. In previous chapters we have hinted at the 'spatial component' which underlies chess skill. One such promising test of it has reached us. In the late 1950s the Czech physiologist and chess trainer Dr Pavel Cerny developed a series of chess aptitude tests (personal communication). One fairly simple one consists of a position with a white knight at a1 and black pawns at c3, c6, f3 and f6 (see diagram).

The task is to move the knight from a1 to b1, then from b1 to c1, and so on all the way along the first rank, visiting each square consecutively. When h1 has been reached, the knight must make its way to a2, then proceed in the same way along the second rank. But at no stage may the knight capture a pawn, nor stand on any square on

which it could be captured. It follows that the second rank tour is a2 to c2 to f2 to h2, and on the third rank c3 and f3 are omitted. The tour is continued until the board has been covered, ending on h8. The task must be performed as rapidly as possible, and then is immediately performed again. The sign of a promising player is either a good first time score (three minutes is grandmaster class, and five minutes is a county player) or a clear improvement from first trial to second trial. A saving of about 25 per cent seems to indicate good learning ability.

This test was performed by a large number of young Czechoslovak players around 1960, and had a good record of success in predicting the future grandmasters among them. Other versions of the test include more complex positions with the pawns replaced by other black pieces. We are reminded of much earlier tasks such as the Knight's Tour, in which a knight has to tour every square on the board without retracing.

In a quite different but equally important field, it is worth mentioning here that Dr Cerny claims to have identified good chess players by physical performance tests. On a cycling exercise machine he has measured the performance of schoolchildren on two tasks: a short sprint task to measure strength, and then a long arduous task for stamina. There were no differences between chess players and non-players on the individual tasks, but the stamina/strength ratio was higher for the chess players.

Pioneering tasks of this kind represent only a fraction of the research which psychologists might devote to chess potential. Arguably, it is important to capture chess talent in the young for training purposes, just as it is vital to foster precocious mathematical ability. Indeed, it is sometimes said that learning chess late in life, e.g.

at adolescence, creates a handicap which is difficult to overcome. Rubinstein became a very great master (with a style of 'refined tranquility'), but he was prone to strange blunders inconsistent with his strength. He learned chess at the age of sixteen. It was not his 'native tongue' said Réti.

In this chapter we have speculated about the origins of skill in different groups. This has given rise to a variety of observations such as 'Russians tend to be good', 'Jews tend to be good', 'Women tend not to be good', and so on. We have tentatively suggested that an interest in chess, and skill in playing it, is related both to a chess tradition in the community and to a variety of social factors. Financial support, whether provided by the State of from private sources, does seem to be a critical factor. And, of course, there are always exceptions, e.g. the spontaneous appearances of Morphy in New Orleans, Capablanca in Cuba and Fischer in Brooklyn. It is just this lack of predictability which makes the sources of genius of such compelling interest.

11 Conclusion

We have examined the problems and sifted the evidence, but are we any closer to producing an Identikit picture of the ideal chess player? We are looking for a man with a dedication to the game which approaches obsession, with the motivation to perform better than his competitors and with that elusive 'chess skill', the ability to recognise the patterns on the chessboard which are the key to deciphering the meaning and potential of the position. Without going any further with our description, we already encounter two major difficulties: chess skill may not exhibit itself in any other sphere of activity, and the high motivation necessary may stem from quite different views of the game. This may explain why widely differing personality types can be seen at the highest levels of chess; men like Tal and Bronstein whose quest for originality brings a mystical element to the game; or Botvinnik, whose relentlessly scientific approach allowed no margin for experimental error; or that growing band of grandmasters for whom chess is simply a profession, to be worked at from nine to five in the periods between tournaments, studying games and positions and perfecting their technique. But there is always room for an exception, perhaps simply a great chess talent who shows no other extraordinary features. Between 1929 and 1933, the chess world was adorned by just such a man.

Sultan Khan was an Indian villager from the Punjab who had shown great ability at chess. The game had a long and respected tradition in his country, but at that time India had no internationally recognised players. The Indian rules also differed slightly from those of the European game. Sultan was encouraged by a wealthy sponsor of chess, Sir Umar Hayat Khan, who brought him to England in 1929. Quickly adapting to the new rules, Sultan Khan won the British

Championship only a few months after his arrival and followed this with tournament successes and excellent performances leading the British Empire team in tournaments. He showed no artistic or cultural interests outside the world of chess, and he was unable to read chess literature, yet within a few years Sultan Khan was established as one of the world's greatest masters. In 1933 he returned with Sir Umar Hayat Khan to India, never to play in another tournament. His ambitions were fully satisfied by farming a small property in his home village, where he lived contentedly until his death in 1966.

Whatever theories one might advance concerning the qualities essential in a great chess player, they would be hard pressed to accommodate the case of Sultan Khan. Perhaps here was a case of pure chess talent, unaccompanied even by the intense love for the game which in most players is too strong for the relationship to be broken. Of course, one cannot attempt to understand such a history without reference to Indian culture. Even so, it is hard to understand how any culture can produce a man with an appetite for chess and for chess success, both of which were satiated after four short years.

If Sultan Khan demonstrated the height of achievement possible on talent alone, we should ask whether such a phenomenon was a symptom of the relatively undeveloped nature of chess at that time, or could a mystic oriental take the chess world by storm even today? Even in his best years, Sultan would occasionally horrify his supporters by his appallingly bad opening play. The level of technique is far higher in the modern game, making it correspondingly more difficult to survive without the benefit of theoretical study.

Have the qualities of the great chess players changed as the game has developed? One may easily suggest natural comparisons which indicate they have not altered much: Morphy and Fischer, Alekhine and Korchnoi, Capablanca and Karpov are pairs from different eras yet with similar personalities (and indeed similar chess styles). How can this be so when the game itself seems to have undergone great changes? The short answer is that the very nature of the game attracts a competitive problem-solving mentality. The working life of the modern grandmaster is very different from that of his predecessors, but the qualities required for success have not changed much. Indeed they are to a large extent those same qualities of dedication and hard work necessary for success in any other field. When we look closely at the work of a modern grandmaster, it is hard to escape the conclusion that nowadays mere talent is not enough. In order to ensure that he stays ahead of potential rivals, world champion Anatoly Karpov estimated that he has to examine around 2,000 grandmaster games each year. For each of those games his task is to assimilate the results of, on average, ten man-hours of grandmaster labour. That is considerably more work than the average top academic has to put in reading relevant papers in journals devoted to his specialist topic. Yet this is a comparatively recent development in the game. Even twenty years ago there were considerably fewer top-class tournaments and consequently fewer games demanding the attention of those wishing to stay at the forefront of knowledge.

Does this mean that chess is becoming more difficult, because it is harder work, or easier because the untalented player now has access to ever increasing libraries of chess knowledge? The true state is a curious mixture of the two. Undoubtedly, now as never before lack of chess talent can be compensated for by application and hard study. Opening systems come ready-packed together with approved middle game strategic plans, and even the endgames which might result have often been analysed in depth before the game begins. The player becomes a technician armed with his manual of other people's ideas. The leading players find increasing difficulty in the task of beating lesser mortals as the average level of technique rises. Chess is a more difficult game now for the player of genuine talent as the technical content rises and opportunities for creative play decrease.

Yet, as every research student knows, a contribution to science need not be a revolutionary new idea. The boundaries of knowledge may always be extended in small ways. As chess knowledge develops, it leaves an increasing number of ragged edges. The creative player will find less scope for dramatic new ideas, but plenty of room for minor innovations. More than fifty years ago, Capablanca suggested that chess was suffering from a 'draw death'. The leading players were toiling away at the same well-known opening systems, they shared the same knowledge, and too many games ended in routine draws. Alekhine exposed the defect in Capablanca's argument by defeating him in a world championship match and leading the way to a new, more dynamic style of play. Chess has lost none of its vitality over the ensuing half-century and looks today as lively as ever.

When he thought that chess was in danger of being played out, Capablanca suggested that it might become necessary to enlarge the board and introduce extra pieces. This raises a fundamental question about chess and its practitioners. What are the essential features of this game which are responsible for its endurance and enormous popularity? And to what extent could we change the rules while preserving its essential character? These questions need to be asked because the rules of chess are highly artificial. We could presumably make small changes in the rules without altering the qualities of the game. If, for example, the rules specified that bishop and knight were transposed in the opening set-up of the pieces, we would still expect Karpov to be the world champion (though if the change were to be made suddenly, the knowledge base of his opening theory would need time to be rebuilt). But what if the original rules had been those of 'randomised chess' in which each game is begun with a random permutation of pieces along the back rank? Then opening theory would never have developed as precisely as it has done today, and there would be considerably less scope for the player of scientific inclination. Probably there would be significant differences in any table of the world's leading players.

It is interesting to speculate about the consequences of such changes in the rules, or in the initial positions of the pieces, but we should certainly not advocate their implementation. As we have made clear throughout this book, the evidence of centuries of practice shows the game to be rich enough for all tastes and strengths. Indeed, there is irony in the fact that Capablanca's proposals were directly motivated by the illusion of invincibility.

We really need a complete taxonomy of human activities to appreciate the true nature of chess. It is a mental exercise, as opposed to physical sports; it is directly competitive, compared, for example, with crossword puzzles; and it is played by an individual, not a team or partnership as in bridge. It is a game of complete information, with the opponent's forces fully visible (unlike poker or bridge again) and, perhaps above all, it is a game where luck is reduced to a minimum, but not totally eliminated. Lastly, chess gives its practitioners a feeling of intellectual productivity unlikely to be equalled in any other game. The geometric beauty of chess ideas exerts a powerful attraction on anyone learning the game and he is hooked by the desire to create something similarly beautiful himself.

The success of the game of chess is quite remarkable. Played in practically every country on earth, it is the most international of all sports. Perhaps we have been lucky that the rules, formulated centuries ago, have withstood both man's and machine's attempts to play perfectly. The game of chess fulfils man's need for direct intellectual competition. Its lasting value owes much to the fact that it is just too difficult for anyone to master it, yet we can all make a fair effort.

And what of the future? Chess is becoming increasingly popular both as a participant and as a spectator sport. The intensity of competition is appreciated by many who do not even play the game themselves. Viewing figures for the BBC *Master Game* and *World Chess Cup* series are known to include many non-players who enjoy the sporting clash of personalities. For those who have previously shunned the unpleasant nature of competition, the easy availability of microprocessors with chess programs has provided them with a ready opponent against whom they can test their ability.

Perhaps chess will have to change to keep pace with technology. When all games are stored on computer files, opening theory will be available at the touch of a button. Preparation for a particular opponent will be considerably eased by asking for a print-out of all his recent games together with all relevant theoretical improvements on his opening play. Already knowledge-based computer programs can play perfectly several endings in which only four or five pieces remain on the board. Will it be fair to adjourn any games in which such endings occur? We can easily foresee a day in the not too distant future when all games will have to be completed in a single session with a consequently faster time-limit than that in general use today. We can also look forward to an answer to at least one of the questions posed in an earlier chapter: whether there is any difference in basic chess ability between men and women. One of the many positive effects of the Women's Liberation movement has been the increasing number of mixed tournaments. A new generation of young women players is emerging who have been brought up in 'unisex' chess. If they can avoid being sidetracked down the cul-de-sac of the women's world championship, they show promising signs of being able to keep pace with their traditionally superior brothers.

One question, however, which will never be answered is the one we posed at the beginning of our discussion of the nature of chess. Is chess a science, an art, a sport, or what? As its popularity grows, the sporting aspects seem to assume greater importance. But the scientific side is always growing as theory accumulates with every tournament which passes; and without the artistry, few would be attracted to the game in the first place. Perhaps David Bronstein will be proved correct in his prediction that chess could be used as a means of communication with other civilisations in space, since we can convey all human emotions through the chessboard. Perhaps, on the other hand, we shall all eventually come to realise, as our non-chess playing loved ones have been trying to tell us for generations, that it is all only a game after all.

Bibliography and References

ABRAHAMS, G. (1951) *The Chess Mind.*
London: English Universities Press

ALEXANDER, C.H.O'D. (1973) *A Book of Chess.*
London: Hutchinson

BARTLETT, F.C. (1932) *Remembering: a study in Experimental and Social Psychology.* Cambridge: C.U.P.

BAUMGARTEN, F. (1939) 'When Samuel Reshevsky was a "Prodigy"', *Chess*, March 1941

BINET, A. (1966) 'Mnemonic virtuosity: a study of chess players', Trans. M.L.Simmel & S.B.Barron, *Genetic Psychology Monographs*, 74, 127-162

BOTVINNIK, M. (1951) 'The Russian and Soviet School of Chess', in *One Hundred Selected Games.* London: Macgibbon and Kee

BOTVINNIK, M. (1981a) *Achieving the Aim.* Oxford: Pergamon

BOTVINNIK, M. (1981b) *Selected Games 1947-70.*
Oxford: Pergamon

BRONSTEIN, D. and SMOLYAN, G. (1982) *Chess in the Eighties.*
Oxford: Pergamon

BRUNER, J.S. (1981) 'The act of discovery',
Harvard Educational Review, 31, 21-32

CHASE, W.G. and SIMON, H.A. (1973) 'Perception in chess', *Cognitive Psychology*, 4, 55-81

CHOMSKY, N. (1957) *Syntactic Structures.* The Hague: Mouton

COCKBURN, A. (1975) *Idle Passion: Chess and the Dance of Death.*
London: Weidenfeld and Nicolson

DE GROOT, A.D. (1965) *Thought and Choice in Chess.*
The Hague: Mouton

DJAKOW, I.N., PETROWSKI, N.V. and RUDIK, P.A.
Psychologie des Schachspiels. Berlin: Walter de Gruyter

DOOLING, D.J. and LACHMAN, R. (1971) 'Effects of
comprehension on retention of prose',
Journal of Experimental Psychology, 88, 216-22

DRAPER, N.R. (1963) 'Does age affect master chess?',
Journal of the Royal Statistical Society, 126, 120-27

DREYFUS, H.L. (1972) *What Computers Can't Do.*
New York: Harper Row

EVANS, J.St.B.T. (1982) *The Psychology of Deductive Reasoning.*
London: Routledge

FINE, R. (1952) *The World's Great Chess Games.* London: Deutsch

FINE, R. (1967) *The Psychology of the Chess Player.*
New York: Dover

FRANKLIN, B. (1786) *The Morals of Chess.*
Philadelphia: Columbian Magazine

GOLOMBEK, H. (1981) *The Penguin Encyclopedia of Chess.*
Harmondsworth: Penguin

GRIS, H. and DICK, W. (1979) *New Soviet Psychic Discoveries.*
London: Souvenir Press

HALLIDAY, J. and FULLER, P. (1974) *Psychology of Gambling.*
London: Allen and Unwin

HARLEY, B. (1931) *Mate in Two Moves: an Introduction to the
Two Move Chess Problem.* London: Bell

HOLDING, D. and REYNOLDS, R. (1982) 'Recall or evaluation
of chess positions as determinants of chess skill',
Memory and Cognition, 10, 237-42

ILYIN-ZHENEVSKY, A.F. (1928) 'The psychology of chess
mistakes', *Shakmatny Listok*, Moscow

JENSEN, A.R. (1980) *Bias in Mental Testing.*
New York: Free Press

JONES, E. (1951) 'The problem of Paul Morphy:
a contribution to the psychology of chess',
Essays in Applied Psychoanalysis, I, 12, 135-64. London: Hogarth

JONES, E. (1954) *Hamlet and Oedipus.* New York: Doubleday

KARPOV, A. (1980) Interview, *AIPE Chess News*, 4, 26

KEENE, R.D. and LEVY, D.N.L. (1970) *Siegen Chess Olympiad.*
Sutton Coldfield: Chess

KOTOV, A. (1975) *Alexander Alekhine.* London: Batsford

KOTOV, A. (1971) *Think like a Grandmaster.* London: Batsford

KOTOV, A. (1981) *Train like a Grandmaster.* London: Batsford

KOTOV, A. and YUDOVICH, M. (1958) *The Soviet School of Chess.*
Moscow: Foreign Languages Publishing House

KRAITCHIK, M. (1943) *Mathematical Recreations.*
London: Allen and Unwin

KROGIUS, N. (1976) *Psychology in Chess.*
New York: R.H.M. Press
KROGIUS, N. (1979) *Chessplayer's Psychological Preparation.*
Moscow
KROGIUS, N. (1981) *The Psychology of Chess Creativity.* Moscow
LASKER, E. (1932) *Lasker's Manual of Chess.*
London: Printing-Craft
LASKER, Ed. (1942) *Chess for Fun and Chess for Blood.*
New York: McKay
MALKIN, V. (1982) 'How to "see" a position', *64*, Moscow
MIESES, J. (1940) 'Psychology and the Art of Chess',
Contemporary Review, 157, 207-13
PAKENHAM-WALSH, R. (1949) 'Chess as a form of recreational
therapy', *Journal of Mental Science*, 95, 203-4
POLUGAYEVSKY, L. (1981) *Grandmaster Preparation.*
Oxford: Pergamon
POPPER, K.R. (1952) *The Open Society and its Enemies. Vol II.
The High Tide of Prophecy: Hegel, Marx and the Aftermath.*
London: Routledge
POPPER, K.R. (1959) *The Logic of Scientific Discovery.*
London: Hutchinson
PUCCETTI, R. (1974) 'Pattern recognition in computers and the
human brain: with special reference to chess playing machines',
British Journal for the Philosophy of Science, 25, 137-54
RETI, R. (1923) *Modern Ideas in Chess.* London: Bell
RETI, R. (1932) *Masters of the Chessboard.*
New York: McGraw Hill
RICHARDS, D.J. (1965) *Soviet Chess.* Oxford: Clarendon Press
RORSCHACH, H. (1932) *Psychodiagnostik.* Berlin: Hans Huber
ROYCROFT, A.J. (1972) *Test Tube Chess.* London: Faber
SIMON, H.A. and GILMARTIN, K. (1973) 'A simulation of
memory for chess positions', *Cognitive Psychology*, 5, 29-46
SMYSLOV, V.V. (1958) *My Best Games of Chess 1935-1957.*
London: Bell
SOLTIS, A. (1976) *The Younger School of Soviet Chess.*
London: Bell
STEINITZ, W. (1889) *The Modern Chess Instructor.*
New York: Putnam
TAL, M. (1976) *The Life and Games of Mikhail Tal.*
New York: R.H.M. Press
TAL, M. (1977) *Tal-Botvinnik World Chess Championship 1960.*
New York: R.H.M. Press

TURING, A.M. (1950) 'Computing machinery and intelligence', *Mind*, 59, 433-60

VASILIEV, L.L. (1963) *Experiments in Mental Suggestion.* London: Institute for the Study of Mental Images

WASON, P.C. (1983) 'Realism and Rationality in the Selection Task', in J.St.B.T.Evans (Ed.) *Thinking and Reasoning: Psychological Approaches.* London: Routledge

WASON, P.C. and JOHNSON-LAIRD, P.N. (1972) *Psychology of Reasoning: Structure and Content.* London: Batsford

WASON, P.C. and REICH, S.S. (1979) 'A verbal illusion', Quarterly Journal of Experimental Psychology, 31, 591-97

WEENINK, H. (1926) *The Chess Problem.* Stroud: Chess Amateur

WOODWORTH, R.S. (1938) *Experimental Psychology.* New York: Holt

ZOBRIST, A.L. and CARLSON, F.R. (1973) 'An advice-taking computer', *Scientific American*, 228, 92-105

ZWEIG, S. (1945) *The Royal Game.* London: Cassell

Index